A NOTE ON THE AUTHOR

LAURIE PENNY was born in London in 1986 and grew up on the Internet. She studied English Literature at Wadham College, Oxford, and in 2010 her blog *Penny Red* was shortlisted for the Orwell Prize for political writing. She is the Contributing Editor at *New Statesman* magazine, Editor-at-Large at the *New Inquiry*, and is known for reporting on protest and social movements. She is the author of *Meat Market: Female Flesh under Capitalism* (2010), a collection of her columns, *Penny Red: Notes from a New Age of Dissent* (2011), and *Discordia: Six Nights in Crisis Athens* (with art by Molly Crabapple, 2012). She currently has some 109,000 followers on Twitter. When she isn't hunched over a laptop, Laurie enjoys lurking in the back of goth clubs and drinking tea with reprobates.

BY THE SAME AUTHOR

Meat Market: Female Flesh under Capitalism

Penny Red: Notes from a new Age of Dissent

Discordia: Six Nights in Crisis Athens
(with Molly Crabapple)

Cybersexism

UNSPEAKABLE THINGS

Sex, Lies and Revolution

Laurie Penny

B L O O M S B U R Y
LONDON • OXFORD • NEW YORK • NEW DELHI • SYDNEY

Bloomsbury Paperbacks
An imprint of Bloomsbury Publishing Plc

50 Bedford Square
London
WC1B 3DP
UK

1385 Broadway
New York
NY 10018
USA

www.bloomsbury.com

First published in Great Britain 2014
This paperback edition first published in 2015

Some parts of the text of this book have been excerpted and extended from articles and blogs written by the author for the *New Statesman* and on her personal blog, www.pennyred.blogspot.com, between 2010 and 2014, and from her article, 'Model Behaviour', first published in the *New Inquiry*, 30 May 2012. Chapter 4, 'Cybersexism', was first published as an eBook in August 2013

British Library Cataloguing-in-Publication Data
A catalogue record for this book is available from the British Library.

ISBN: TPB: 978-1-4088-2474-0
PB: 978-1-4088-5769-4
ePub: 978-1-4088-2608-9

2 4 6 8 10 9 7 5 3 1

Typeset by Hewer text UK Ltd, Edinburgh
Printed and bound in Great Britain by CPI Group (UK) Ltd, Croydon CR0 4YY

For Roz Kaveney

and

for G. E. B. and E. K. P.

Please hold my handbag, I'm wrestling the angel
That's nesting like a hen in the corner of my life.
She bends to me and simpers – will you never change, girl?
You can't change this strange world. Why not be a wife?

Sophia Blackwell, 'Wrestling the Angel',
Into Tempatation

Fuck heroes, fight now

graffiti, Athens 2011

CONTENTS

Acknowledgements

So many people have given time and energy to this project that I can only hope it's halfway worthy of their efforts. Thanks go, firstly, to my agent, the magical Juliet Pickering at Blake Friedmann, for all her hard work. To Bill Swainson, who always believed in this book, and to Sophia, Oliver and everyone at Bloomsbury. To Helen Lewis at the *New Statesman*, and Jason Cowley, who gave me my start.

Endless thanks, too, to Cath Howdle, Charlie Hallam, Zoe Stavri, Adrian Bott, Natasha Lennard, James Butler, Nick Lezard, Richard Seymour, Maria Dahvana Headley, Mariya Protzenko, China Miéville, Rachel Rosenfelt, Jed Weightman, Leigh Alexander, Kitty Stryker, Willow Brugh, Clay Shirky, G. Balfe, Jo Afiya W, Benjamin Baker, Katrina Duncan, Neil Girling, Kiera James, Eleanor Saitta, Meredith Yayanos and Emma Felber, friends who held me up in hard times and gave vital feedback on early drafts. So did Janice Cable, who made a home for me when I ran away to New York to write – and I'm grateful for her wisdom, beauty and tolerance for loud late-night tea-making. Paul Mason was the friend and mentor every young journalist dreams of having, but few are lucky enough to find.

Stoya, Buck Angel, Akynos Shekera, Cindy Gallop, Meg Barker and Kate Bornstein lent their time and insight as interviewees. Molly Crabapple, my muse and hero, let me crash on her carpet over countless nights drinking espressos and arguing sex and syntax, and like any true friend, she never let me give up. Nor did Roz Kaveney, poet, philosopher, activist, wicked auntie, fairy godmother, to whom these pages are dedicated. My mum brought me up to be brave, and put up with me not doing my fair share of the Christmas washing-up because I had deadlines. My baby sisters inspire me to keep fighting every day. Our dad, Raymond Barnett (1948–2013), never got to see this book finished, but I owe him everything. Thanks, Dad. I love you.

Introduction

This is not a fairy tale.

This is a story about how sex and money and power put fences around our fantasies. This is a story about how gender polices our dreams. Throughout human history, the most important political battles have been fought on the territory of the imagination, and what stories we allow ourselves to tell depend on what we can imagine.

Women, like any oppressed class, learn to fear our own rage. Our anger is legitimately terrifying. We know that if it ever gets out, we might get hurt, or worse, abandoned. One sure test of social privilege is how much anger you get to express without the threat of expulsion, arrest, or social exclusion, and so we force down our rage like rotten food until it festers and sickens us.

This is a feminist book. It is not a cheery instruction manual for how to negotiate modern patriarchy, with a sassy wink and a thumbs-up. It is not a charming, comforting book about sex and shopping and shoes. I am unable to write any such thing. I cannot force a smile for you. As a handbook for happiness in a fucked-up world, this book cannot be trusted.

Nor is this an academic study – it's a polemic grounded in research, experience and years of writing and campaigning on the queer and feminist scenes in Britain and America and online. I have seen enough women shamed for speaking of rape or threatened with death for seeking basic reproductive healthcare; enough men beaten or bullied to suicide for not acting straight enough; enough people of both sexes and every gender driving themselves to despair in order to live up to stereotypes of success that they never chose.

This is a book about love and sex in austerity, about gender under neoliberalism. 'Neoliberalism' refers to the attempt to reorganise society and the state on the basis of an ideal of 'the market'. Neoliberalism proclaims that the logic of business and money is the best determinant of human happiness. Neoliberalism also says that human beings can't be trusted, so the market must necessarily dictate what the people want. Every category of human interaction, therefore – from the public sector to the intimate adventures of love and lust – must be made to work more like a market, with in-built competitive mechanisms and cost controls. Every personal choice, including democratic choice, must be subsumed into the logic of the market: flesh itself can be remoulded for profit.

We are told that this is what liberty looks like. Neoliberalism is an attempt to build a 'Machinery of Freedom', in the words of David Friedman, in which human beings are economic creatures first and foremost. Everything we do should be about 'maximising utility', whether it's in a relationship, in a job, or in social situations. The self is just an entrepreneurial project. The body is just human capital, a set of resources – whether the brain, the breasts or the biceps – which can be put to work generating an income stream.

This affects everyone – but women most of all. Women are more likely than men to perform labour that is socially necessary but low waged or unwaged, and more likely to need public services and welfare. In this nominally freer and more equal world, most women end up doing more work, for less reward, and feeling pressured to conform more closely to gender norms.

Neoliberalism, while extolling the 'career woman', reviles poor women, women of colour, sex workers and single mothers as hopeless dependants, sluts and thieves. That's why the 'career woman' is a neoliberal hero: she triumphs on the market's own terms without overturning any hierarchies.

The 'career woman' is the new aspirational ideal for young girls everywhere: she is a walking CV, her clothing, make-up and cosmetic-surgery choices merely means of upgrading her 'erotic capital' to generate more income for herself or her boss. She is always beautiful, invariably white, and almost entirely fictional. Nonetheless, it is her freedom that is prioritised, as states across the world cut services and provisions for poor women while championing the cause of 'women in boardrooms'.[1] Neoliberalism colonises our dreams. It cannibalises our ideals of freedom and regurgitates them as strategies of social control.

This is a feminist book in that it raises feminist politics as a solution to the colonisation of the most essential of our passions by money and hegemony. It also has dirty bits. If you're only interested in those, skip to pages 231–4.

I started writing this book in the middle of a student occupation, curled up with the laptop on my knees while young people staggered in bruised and shaken, having seen their friends cuffed and beaten for daring to stand in front of their parliament building and demand a better future. I wrote the rest in notebooks, in strange apartments above occupied public squares as police and protesters clashed on the wasted dreamscapes of neoliberalism. I watched the young naive middle-class women and men of the twenty-first century learn the true nature of the world they live in. I watched all this happening, and I believe that there is hope. I believe that if anything can save us in this fraught and dazzling future, it is the rage of women and girls, of queers and freaks and sinners. I believe that the revolution will be feminist, and that when it comes it will be more intimate and more shocking than we have dared to imagine.

This book will not help you find a man, fix your hair or keep your job. This is a book about love and sex, beauty and disgust, power and passion and technology. It is a book about the intimate territory of unrest. I wrote it in unfamiliar cities, in conversation with teenage runaways, radical feminists, anarchists, hipster kids, sex workers, mad artists, convicted criminals, transsexual activists and sad young women in small towns longing for adventure.

This is for the others, as one of the others, as one of those who will never be satisfied with good enough, with free enough, with equality for some. This is for the unspeakable ones, the unnatural ones, the ones who upset people. Who do not do as they are told. Who speak when they shouldn't and refuse to smile when they are supposed on demand. Who are weird and always want too much. If you're one of those, or think you might be, this book's for you.

WHAT MORE ARE YOU AFTER?

Why does mainstream feminism remain so tepid and cowardly?

The notion that feminism matters and has much work to do is no longer a minority opinion. After decades of tentative acquiescence, women and girls and their allies across the world have begun to speak out to demand a better deal, not just in law but in practice. They have begun to challenge rape culture, slut-shaming, sexual violence. They have begun to fight for reproductive injustice and against the systemic poverty that has always fallen heaviest on women and particularly upon mothers.[2] As finance capitalism faltered following the near-collapse of the global stock markets in 2008, the notion that one day all women would be able to make empowering choices within a market that respected their goals and autonomy was exposed as a twenty-year-old fairy tale.

The feminism that has mattered to the media and made magazine headlines in recent years has been the feminism most useful to heterosexual, high-earning middle- and upper-middle-class white women. Public 'career feminists' have been more concerned with getting more women into 'boardrooms', when the problem is that there are altogether too many boardrooms, and none of them are on fire.

There was an understanding that gender liberation, like wealth, would somehow 'trickle down'.[3] The flaw in this plan, of course, was that it was arrant bollocks. Feminism, like wealth, does not trickle down, and while a small number of extremely privileged women worry about the glass ceiling, the cellar is filling up with water, and millions of women and girls and their children are crammed in there, looking up as the flood creeps around their ankles, closes around their knees, inches up to their necks.

Just when it should be most radical, 'public feminism' has become increasingly concerned with a species of thin-lipped censoriousness that posits sex, rather than sexism, as the real problem. The feminist campaigns that attract the most attention and funding are those concerned with stamping out pornography, ending prostitution and preventing the sale of suggestive T-shirts.[4]

This is a discourse that treats women as victims not just of our admittedly hugely fucked-up erotic culture, but of sex itself, without properly understanding the nature of commercial sexuality or of objectification. Sexism is apparently not the problem: the problem is sex, the nature of it, the amount of it that's being had away from moralising eyes, sometimes for money.

We were lied to. The women of my generation were told that we could 'have it all', as long as 'it all' was marriage, babies and a career in finance, a cupboard full of beautiful shoes and terminal exhaustion – and even that is only an option if we're rich, white, straight and well behaved. These perfect lives would necessarily rely on an army of nannies and care-workers, and nobody has yet bothered to ask whether they can have it all.

We can have everything we want as long as what we want is a life spent searching for exhausting work that doesn't pay enough, shopping for things we don't need and sticking to a set of social and sexual rules that turn out, once you plough through the layers of trash and adverts, to be as rigid as ever.

As for young men, they were told they lived in a brave new world of economic and sexual opportunity, and if they felt angry or afraid, if they felt constrained or bewildered by contradictory expectations, by the pressure to act masculine, make money, demonstrate dominance and fuck a lot of pretty women while remaining a decent human being, then their distress was the fault of women and minorities. It was these grasping women, these homosexuals and people of colour who had taken away the power and satisfaction that was once their birthright as men. We were taught, all of us, that if we were dissatisfied, it was our fault, or the fault of those closest to us. We were built wrong, somehow. We had failed to adjust. If we showed any sort of distress, we probably needed to be medicated or incarcerated, depending on our social status. There are supposed to be no structural problems, just individual maladaption.

The world has changed for women and queers as much as it possibly could without upsetting the underlying structure of society, which is still sexist, homophobic and misogynist, because it relies for its continued existence on sexual control, on social inequality and on the unpaid labour of women and girls. Further change will require more ambition than we have hitherto been permitted. Further change will require us to speak what is unspoken, to refuse to accept the world as it is. It will require us to ask big, challenging questions about the nature of work and love, sex and politics, and to be prepared for the answers to be different from what we had expected. That is what this book attempts to do.

I am twenty-seven years old; I do not know all the answers. But I think I know some of the questions, and it is questions that interest me more.

Asking questions is the authority of the young, and it's the first thing girls are told not to do. Don't put your hand up in class, or the boys will shout you down. Don't talk back to your teachers, to your parents, to the police. Asking questions is dangerous.

For forty thousand years of human history, biology divided men and women into different sex classes and rigid gender roles. Then, two or three generations ago – an eyeblink in the long dream of human history – technology moved forwards and allowed women to escape the constraints of reproductive biology just after movements across the world had succeeded in gaining them the right to be considered full citizens in law. That sexual revolution became a social revolution, and the shape of human relations was changed for ever. It can't be undone. Women will not return to sexual and political subjection without a fight to the death. But some people are still unaccountably angry that that sweeping social change was ever thought of, and have hung screaming on to our ankles every step of the long, slow trudge to gender equality. We are not there yet.

Right now a counter-revolution is under way against many of the gains that women have won, at great cost, over centuries of backlash and violence and ridicule. The counter-revolution is a social one, an economic one and a sexual one. This is a new culture war, a sexual counter-revolution. It is much bigger than the tactical 'war on women' that was briefly reported in the United States in the run-up to the presidential elections of 2012, as Republican lawmakers lost their collective wits in a moral meltdown over rape, contraception and abortion.[5] That this sexual counter-revolution will never fully succeed makes it no less likely to ruin lives and destroy progress, nor does it dent the overwhelming message of those who seek to restrict women's socio-sexual choices in the twenty-first century. The message is: thus far, and no further.

FEMINISM IS FOR EVERYONE

Every few months, it seems, the media rediscovers feminism and decides it's a trendy new way to sell books and magazines, as long as it doesn't scare people by posing any actual threat to their way of life. The sort of feminism that sells is the sort of feminism that can appeal to almost everybody while challenging nobody, feminism that soothes, that speaks for and to the middle class, aspirational feminism that speaks of shoes and shopping and sugar-free snacks and does not talk about poor women, queer women, ugly women, transsexual women, sex workers, single parents, or anybody else who fails to fit the mould. That sort of feminism does not interest me. Let others write it. Let others construct an unchallenging feminism that speaks only to the smallest common denominator.[6] The young women of today know far better than their slightly older sisters who came of age in the listless 1990s how much work is still to be done, and how unglamorous much of it is. They know how bloody important it is to talk about power, and class, and work, and love, race and poverty and gender identity.

This book is the start of one such conversation, and if that conversation included only women with absolutely similar backgrounds to my own it would not be worth having. At the same time, I'm aware that I can't know everything. The fact that I was born white and middle class in an English-speaking country and form relationships mostly although not exclusively with men inevitably affects how I think, how I write, and how I live my life. I am not writing as Everygirl, because there's no such thing.

Too many feminist writers attempting the 'book as bombshell' approach to a theory of gender and power begin with the disclaimer that they cannot possibly say anything about women who are not white, or straight, or rich, or cissexual,[7] or mothers, or employed as full-time writers in London or New York City. That's their experience, and they can't speak for anyone else, which means they don't have to bother talking to anyone else or reading what anybody else has written, unless those writers are straight, white, wealthy, married professionals, too.

Hey, girls, we're all the same in the end, aren't we?

The idea that there is any such thing as Everygirl, a 'typical' woman who can speak to and for every other person on the planet in possession of a vagina, is one of the major sexist fairy tales of our time. Patriarchy tends to see all women as alike; it would prefer that we were all interchangeable rich, pretty, white, baby-making straight girls whose problems revolve around how to give the best blow jobs and where to buy diet pills. No man would ever be expected to write a book speaking to and for all men everywhere just because he happens to have a cock. The original feminist statement that the personal is political[8] has been undermined by the insistence, in every media industry still run and owned by powerful men, that all women's politics be reduced to the purely personal.[9]

Whoever we are, our understanding of gender, politics and feminism is going to be conditioned by our experience of love and sex, especially if we are straight. When we speak of fighting sexism, whether we know it or not, we're bringing our broken hearts to the table, we're bringing our wounded pride to the table, all those stomach-twisting sexual rejections, our frustration, our loneliness and longing, the memory of betrayal, the pain of our childhoods. We're also bringing the anxious heat of our desire, our passion for our friends and partners and children, every time a lover has laid a hand softly over a part of your soul you didn't know was stinging and soothed it. All of that at once, and more, and more, because gender politics are personal as well as political, but that doesn't mean the political has to collapse into the personal.

LET'S NOT TALK ABOUT BOYS AND GIRLS LIKE THAT'S A THING

Women. Men. Boys and girls. The words don't change but the resonance does, and what it means to call yourself one of those things in the twenty-first century is something very different from what it meant in the last century and what it will mean in the next. Being a woman, or being a man, requires effort, attention, the suppression of some parts of your personality and the exaggeration of others. When Simone de Beauvoir said that 'one is not born, but rather becomes, a woman' she was bang on, but I prefer Bette Davis in the film *All About Eve*, reminding us that 'That's one career all females have in common, whether we like it or not – being a woman. Sooner or later we've got to work at it, no matter how many other careers we've had or wanted.'

Gender identity is work, performance work, a job we got signed up to involuntarily from the day someone held us up to the light and described our nether regions to our gasping mothers. Women, in particular, must perform femininity as part of our work if we want to be paid, or protected, or to retain whatever dignity and standing we've managed to rip from the rough surface of the society we're stuck in. Let's be clear: when I talk about 'being a woman' or 'being a man', I'm not talking about biological sex, but social role. From birth and through childhood human beings are segregated by sex and made suspicious of one another: compliance with norms of masculinity and femininity, from how to dress and who to kiss to what team sports you're supposed to follow, is enforced, often with physical violence, and those who cannot or will not fit in have to work it out alone.

Not everyone identifies with the sex they were assigned at birth. A significant minority of human beings are transsexual, transgender, genderqueer or intersex, and their experience of what gender means has traditionally been either excluded from mainstream feminist discussion or actively attacked. Not everyone, moreover, identifies strongly as a man or a woman, and not all of those who do feel a particular compulsion to dress or behave in a certain way in order to be tolerated, respected, rewarded at home and promoted and protected in public.

There is still something, though, that puts those of us who were born or became women in a special predicament. And there is something about that predicament that informs the totality of gender oppression. It is important that everyone understands how sexism affects women and thereby impacts on all human beings. Women are subject to stricter rules of behaviour: how to act, what to say, what to want. What to wear, what to eat, where to shop, how to behave at work, when not to text him back, when to fuck, how to fuck, what colour to put in your hair when he leaves you. If you took the adverts out of what the mainstream media still thinks of as its 'women's content', lists of instructions is almost all there would be left. It is hard to be a man, in this world, and it is harder still to be a woman, to be of the class that is meant to bear all the violence and trauma that society inflicts on men and then to bear the fallout of men's trauma, too, smoothing their brows, sucking their dicks, suffering their gendered violence with the gentle subservience in which we are trained from birth.

Gender is a straitjacket for the human soul.[10] Gender works us all over, makes enemies of the people we're supposed to love, and it works women over the most. We are the ones for whom biology is not just destiny: it is catastrophe.

We still aren't happy, not women, not men, and some people will tell you that's because of feminism, and some will say that it's in spite of feminism. I'd argue that it's because the fight against capitalist patriarchy has barely begun, but what we know for sure is that there's something about gender roles, man and woman, boy and girl, that makes people desperately unhappy. We know this because gender is still the main language we use to discuss existential crises.

Women are more depressed than men, more anxious than men, use twice as much psychiatric medication and are three times as likely as men to attempt suicide. Men, however, are twice as likely to succeed in the attempt.[11] Men's emotional and psychological trauma is more likely to be untreated, to be borne in silence and nursed in private until a sudden snapping point is reached where the heart can take no more and you turn on yourself violently, finally, with a rope, with a knife, with your father's gun. Most of the cultural narrative around mental health right now revolves around gender, with scientists and social theorists trying to work out whether it's men or women who are more distressed, and whose fault that might be. Precisely who is more fucked up, boys or girls, has never been conclusively decided, but the fact that we insist on trying to work it out reveals a truth: there is something about gender right now that is deeply troubling, on an intimate level that is rarely discussed. There is something about the experience of being a woman or being a man, or of trying to be a woman or trying to be a man in the twenty-first century that many people find profoundly distressing in a way that they find difficult to speak about even in those few spaces where they are allowed to.

Have we upset the natural order of things?

YOU MAKE ME FEEL LIKE AN UNNATURAL WOMAN

Wherever there is anxiety to stop the world from changing too much or changing at all, we still find ourselves told that such-and-such a change is 'unnatural'. Expecting real equality for women in the workplace is 'unnatural' – nature wants women to clock out of public life when and if they have kids, and if they don't want to have kids, they must be unnatural. Women who are ambitious and independent are unnatural. Women who actively express sexual desire are unnatural. Women refusing to make themselves pretty and pleasing for men are unnatural. Women who demand respect and security while not being beautiful and young are unnatural. Abortion is unnatural. Contraception is unnatural. Pleasure for its own sake is unnatural.

Unnatural, in short, covers a lot of the fun stuff.

But rape, though, rape is natural. Male violence against women is natural. Homophobia is natural. Discrimination against queer women, poor women, black women, fat women, ugly women, trans women and feminine men is natural. Poverty is natural, especially when the poor are mothers with young children and no men around. That's just the way the world works. Death in childbirth is natural. Making women pay a higher social price for sexual pleasure is natural. Sexual double standards are natural; women have been less free, less powerful and more exploited than men for centuries, and maybe there's been a little bit of progress, but we really shouldn't ask for any more. Asking for more is unnatural. Bitches ought to know their place.

The question, of course, is: why the fuck would anyone want to be natural?

For fifty years, patriarchy has been telling women to get back to the kitchen, first in genuine outrage, and then with the type of ironic crypto-sexism that is supposed to be amusing: get back in there and make us a sandwich, dear. Those who are so eager for women and girls to go back to the kitchen might think again about just what it is we might be up to in there. You can plan a lot of damage from a kitchen. It's also where the knives are kept.

The truth is that there is nothing 'natural' about what it means to be a man or a woman today. Gender identity is performed, and it is performed for profit, whether social, financial or personal. That performance is an adaptive strategy for dealing with overwhelmingly hostile territory. Now we need to adapt again. And that's what feminism is: adaptation. Evolution.

Feminism is not a set of rules. It is not about taking rights away from men, as if there were a finite amount of liberty to go around. There is an abundance of liberty to be had if we have the guts to grasp it for everyone. Feminism is a social revolution, and a sexual revolution, and feminism is in no way content with a missionary position. It is about work, and about love, and about how one depends very much on the other. Feminism is about asking questions, and carrying on asking them even when the questions get uncomfortable.

For example. A question about whether men and women should be paid equally for equal work leads to another about what equal work really means when most domestic and caring jobs are still done by women for free, often on top of full-time employment. The answers to that lead to a whole new set of questions about what work should be paid, and what is simply a part of love and duty, and then you start questioning the nature of love itself, and that's when it really starts to get uncomfortable.

The confinement of women to the home has never just been a middle-class experience. However, some of the earliest Second-Wave feminism, starting with Betty Friedan's *The Feminine Mystique*, spoke chiefly of the plight of the suburban wife and mother, her frustration and neurosis, her longing to escape her endless rotation of dishes and dinner-dates and salon gossip to the male world of work and power from which she was excluded. That pain – the torment of the middle-class housewife longing for an office job – has been allowed to define the popular understanding of what feminism is for, and what women really want, for two generations. The fact that outside white suburbia women have always had to work for money does not factor into this convenient fiction. The fantasy that all women really need in order to be equal and contented is to be permitted to work for pay, while continuing to perform their duties in the home – an exhausting schedule of self-negation that we now speak of as 'having it all'. 'Having it all' now means having a career, kids, a husband, a decent blow-dry – and that's it.

Work itself has been repurposed as women's liberation. However unsatisfying and badly paid, if you've got a job, you're a free bitch, baby. Anyone who has actually done a day's work knows that this is a cyclopean lie. Nonetheless, women's liberation has been redefined as absolute conformity to contemporary standards of femininity, at best a conformity that requires endless work, constant disappointment, a conformity that is no sure route to health and happiness even for those who have the means to pursue it. Modern do-it-all superwomen are so knackered and seething that they have started baking stacks of silly little biscuits and flouncing about in retro 1950s-print dresses as if doing so might bring back the days when you still had to do the shopping, the cooking and the squeezing out of babies but if you were very lucky and very pretty you might be able to persuade a man to cover the finances, because the further away from it some of us get the better that option is starting to look.

The past is a different country: people are always laying claim to it in the name of one ideology or another, with no regard for the people that actually live there. For women and girls in the West, recent history has been colonised by the notion that previous generations of females were not free chiefly because they could not work for a wage. In the modern fantasy of the 1950s, women were confined to the home, to the kitchen sink and the picket fence and the husband and kids. For a great many exhausted modern women, this gilded fairy-tale cage is probably rather appealing: spending your days fussing around the house and watching your kids grow up is hardly less dignified than trekking daily to an office job that pays you less than the cost of a two-room flat. If all feminism won for us is the right to work, you could be forgiven for feeling that maybe gender liberation isn't all it's cracked up to be, that maybe the women who plumped for the handsome prince and housewifery had the right idea all along.

Femininity as it is currently conceived is entrepreneurial, and it is competitive: hack social theorists like Catherine Hakim speak without irony of women's 'erotic capital',[12] in a manner which is only repulsive because it makes explicit what is so often said out of the corners of the mouths of parents and teachers and girlfriends: your femininity is a brand, your eroticism your best money in the bank, to be held and cashed in when it is of most value. Your very gender identity, one of the most intimate parts of what makes you yourself, is entirely for sale, or should be. This is one of the reasons why women, and particularly young women, have adapted particularly well to the way in which social media and the capitalisation of the social realm requires everyone to apply the logic of branding to our own lives in order to gain followers. We have always been encouraged to understand femininity as a form of branding, albeit one burnt into our flesh at birth.

Work, beauty and romance, then marriage, mortgage and kids: that definition of total freedom has been allowed to conquer our imaginations, leaving no space for any other lives. But what if you want something else? Is that still allowed?

WHAT DO YOU WANT TO WANT?

The girl in green at the back of the room has had her hand up for fifteen minutes. Her arm is weakening and she's having to hold it up with the other hand. She cannot be more than twenty. She has the sort of pale, flowy princess hair that I used to long for as a child, the sort of hair that makes you want to touch it to see if it's really as soft as it looks, the sort of hair that would stream behind you when you run, that belongs to the sort of girl who's never supposed to run anywhere. We're in a university lecture room in Germany, and I've been invited to speak about gender and desire like I know the answers.

The girl with the princess hair has that flush in her face that men write longingly of because it implies both youth and shame. She is the sort of girl that writers of every gender describe at length and don't bother to listen to. She is the sort of girl who sits at the back waiting for her turn to ask a question and does not complain when her turn does not come, except that this time it does, and it's this:

'What do I want?'

I ask her to repeat that, please. I'm not sure I've heard correctly.

'My question is, what do I really want? You talk about what women want and what we are told to want like there's a difference. I know in my heart that I want to be free and independent. But I also want to be beautiful, and have a boyfriend, and please my parents, and do everything the magazines say. So how do I know if what I want is what I really want? And what should I want?'

Well, isn't that the question. What are we supposed to want? What should we want, as girls, as boys, as humans fighting for identity and power when we're supposed to stay in neat lines of behaviour based on biology? What do we get to want from each other and from our lives?

Desire is a social idea. It has taken me until I'm almost out of the official part of my youth even to work out what I want to want.

I can tell you what we're supposed to want: hard work, bland beauty and romance leading to money, marriage and kids: the definition of total freedom that has been allowed to conquer our imaginations, leaving no space for any other lives. But what if we want something else? Is that still allowed?

What if we want freedom?

MUTINY IN OUR TIME?

There comes a time when you have to decide whether to change yourself to fit the story, or change the story itself. The decision gets a little easier if you understand that refusing to shape your life and personality to the contours of an unjust world is the best way to start creating a new one.

There comes a time when you have to decide what you will permit yourself to want.

While we're on the subject, here's what I want. I want mutiny. I want women and queers and everyone else who's been worked over by gender and poverty and power, which by the way means most of us, to stop waiting to be rewarded for good behaviour. There are no gold stars coming and there are few good jobs left. Even if we buy the right clothes and work the right hours and show up every day with the same cold gag of a smile clenched between our teeth, there's no guarantee we'll be left alone to grow old before the floodwaters come in.

Forget it. It's done. The social revolution that's been choking and stumbling down a gauntlet of a century and more, the feminist fightback, the sexual re-scripting, the tearing up of old norms of race and class and gender, it has to start again, with all of us this time, not just the rich white kids who needed it least. So it has to be mutiny.

It must be mutiny. Nothing else will do. I used to be less hardline about this. I used to vote, and sign petitions, and argue for change within the system. I stayed up all night to watch Obama get elected; I cheered for the Liberals in London. I thought that maybe if we kept asking for small change – a shift in attitudes about body hair, a slight increase in the minimum wage, maybe shut down a few porn shops and let the gays marry – then eventually we'd get the little bit of freedom we wanted, if it wasn't too much trouble.

No more of that. Being a good girl gets you nowhere. Asking nicely for change gets you nowhere. Mutiny is necessary. Class mutiny, gender mutiny, sex mutiny, love mutiny. It's got to be mutiny in our time.

We're encouraged to feel sympathetic only towards the people who have traditionally held power in society – men, white people, straight people, the upper classes – for graciously giving away a tiny bit of their privilege, scraps of opportunity for the rest of us to share. We're told that equality on paper, equality in a court of law, is enough in a society whose laws have always been applied unfairly and pursued unequally. Most of all we're told that this is enough. There can be no better world than the one we're living in now. We learn that equality, social opportunity and personal and sexual freedom are luxuries that society can't afford. But it's not true. Liberty cannot be crafted in a court of law alone. This isn't the sexual revolution we were told was over and done with. This isn't where feminism finished. This is where it starts.

Or maybe I'm wrong. Maybe this really is as good as it gets. Maybe history did end in 1989[13] and we're all going to have to put up with the way things are. Maybe we're happy that so many girls grow up scared and abused, that so many women are obliged to carve themselves up and shut themselves down and be beautiful and silent until men have no use for them any more, that so many men and boys are helped to build a box of violence and inertia to keep their pain and rage in and quietly taught to lock the door from the inside. Maybe a bit of us likes it better that way.

So here's the deal. I'm not going to tell you how to be a better version of what you already are. I'm not going to lay out yet another set of rules for how to behave, or how to make nice, or how to be the best girl you can be. And I swear to you, I absolutely promise, I'm not going to tell you whether or not to shave your pubic hair or judge you on the state of your armpits. I could not give a damn about your furze or lack of it.

Nor is this yet another guidebook for navigating the treacherous machine of patriarchy when what we should be doing is smashing the machine and quitting the factory with as many of our loved ones as we can grab. The world doesn't need another handbook for how to submit with dignity to a world that wants you to hate yourself. Women and girls in particular don't need any more rules for living and working and grooming and loving. There are already too many rules, most of them contradictory. I've been reading those glossy guidebooks since I was five years old along with a load-bearing amount of feminist theory, and I've still got no idea how to be a good girl, and if I did, I wouldn't tell you.

I'm not here to tell you how to be a feminist, or whether you should be one at all. I call myself a feminist to fuck with people, and because it's a great way to weed out the creeps in bars, but feminism isn't an identity. Feminism is a process. Call yourself what you like. The important thing is what you fight for. Begin it now.

I

Fucked-Up Girls

They will love me for that which destroys me.
Sarah Kane, *4.48 Psychosis*

The carpet is the colour of nasal mucus and stinks of bleach. I know this because I have my face pressed into it, and while trying to keep still enough that the nurses don't find me I examine the eerie snot-shade of the rug, human head-dirt scrubbed down to the grain like everything else in this hospital ward. Not a crumb of dust or a smudge of grease is permitted in this place where even kindness is as clinical and smothering as a disinfected blanket. I'm seventeen years old, and I'm hiding under the bed.

It's 2004, and I should be at school, studying for my exams. Instead I'm in a mental unit for people with life-threatening anorexia, investing my energy in new ways to keep out of sight of the nurses who come around every ten minutes, day and night, to check that you haven't thrown up your protein powder or smashed a CD and used the shards to slice words of anger deep, deep into the flesh of your forearms. Both of these things have happened in recent weeks. I remember the last one because it was my roommate and my Sleater-Kinney CD she used. I haven't got anything so exotic planned. I just want to be alone with my notebook for more than ten minutes at a time, left alone with my thoughts where nobody can look at me.

Hence the hiding under the bed, shivering. There's a fine down of mossy hair growing on my back, which is something that happens when you're dangerously underweight and live in a cold country. Your body tries to keep itself warm any way it can.

So you hunch up by radiators, shaking uncontrollably, trying to fight off a chill that has shoved its icy-cold fingers into your bones, trying and failing. Your personality leaches away. You have become a creature that starves and shits and pukes and shivers and that's about it. You can't think straight. Your appearance terrifies your friends and family. Lack of nutrients means you run on adrenalin and you become a primitive thing hunting despite itself for food of any sort, rifling through bins, shoving handfuls of cereal into your face only to throw it all up in a panic. You're a mess. Your hair thins and falls out. You do sit-ups and push-ups compulsively, run for miles a day on half a cup of weak oatmeal.

You do not do this to look beautiful. You know you look like hell. You do it because you want to disappear. You don't want to be looked at any more. You're sick of being looked at and judged and found wanting. You don't want to grow up and fill out and engage with sex in a way that's healthy and positive. Above all, you're sick of being watched. You've done everything you can to be good and you've still failed, and now you're just another fucked-up white girl circling the drain.

Fucked-up white girls. The bookshelves and magazine racks in every major city are stuffed with stories about fucked-up white girls, beautiful broken dollies, unable to cope with the freedom and the opportunities they've inherited, poor things. We fetishise an idea of these girls, photograph them, airbrush out the distended bellies and jutting bones, add sparkle to the dull skin and glazed-over features, wash them out with the lights of clicking cameras as if all the old suspicions were true and those beetle-black machines were stealing their souls snap by snap by snap. Not coping has become a fashion accessory, an indulgence. It's cool not to cope. The coke habit, the booze problem, the eating disorder, the paper-thin transcendent beauty of the young woman rich enough to know that there'll be a support system in place if she ever reaches the point of total collapse: it's become part of the neoliberal mythos of womanhood, and the consumption – the young girl driven to distraction until she starts consuming herself, bone feeding on muscle feeding on bad drugs and narcissism, gorgeous neurosis – is the apex and embodiment of what women are supposed to be, what modern life is supposed to be: we eat ourselves from within. We strive for perfection, and we are perfectly miserable. Having it all is no longer expected to include personal fulfilment. That's what the shops are for.

Falling apart elegantly is a rich girl's game, a white girl's game, a fashion girl's game. That's what the celebrity magazines would have you believe. It's all bullshit, of course. When you get down to the meat and snot and bones of the situation, precisely nobody seems interested in the interiority of the fucked-up girl, the unglamorous, everyday breakdowns, the real struggle to adjust to the pressures and contradictions and everyday humiliations that constitute female reality in the twenty-first-century West, not just in Chelsea and the Upper West Side, but for all of us. In real life, girls from all backgrounds, in suburbs and ghettos and rural backwaters and in the Global South, are just as likely to flake out, swallow their rage and take it out on their bodies, and everywhere it's getting worse.[1] There's even a word for this now, a new clinical diagnosis, slapped on women far more often than men: adjustment disorder.[2] You have failed to adjust adequately to social expectations.

TAKING UP SPACE

Eight years later. It's springtime in New York City. The girl at the table opposite me is doing something very strange with her sandwich. She has cut it into exact quarters and is slowly, gingerly dissecting each one as if it were a bomb about to go off, removing the bread, wiping off the mayonnaise with a paper towel, piling the meat and lettuce into precise piles with a tiny scrape of mustard and eating them hurriedly, her hands trembling. You might expect the other people in the café to notice, but this is New York, where the spectacle of hungry, pool-eyed young women ritually starving themselves has become routine.

I watch the girl reflected in the glass of the café window. I have nothing in common with her except that we happen to be the same person. Or rather, we were, a lifetime ago this week when I was admitted to hospital with anorexia. It's three years since I made a full recovery, but now and then around this time of year, the old, weird habits creep back: food the enemy, every mirror a traitor. I don't know quite what happened to the skinny, miserable seventeen-year-old I used to be. Over the long months of learning that it was all right to take up space, I suspect I may have eaten her. But I see people just like her every day on the streets of every major city, ghost people with mad eyes staring blankly ahead, spindly limbs pistoning with manic energy, wrapped up against a chill that can't be fought, and they include women of all ages, and at least 15 per cent of them are men.

Eating disorders are still seen as diseases peculiar to pretty young white women, which perhaps explains why years of 'awareness raising' have led to a great deal of glamour and mystery surrounding this deadliest of mental illnesses and precious little understanding. After thousands of histrionic articles conveniently illustrated with pictures of half-naked models looking upset, the number of people with eating disorders is still rising, and we are no closer to solving one of the great mysteries of modern life – namely, why so many of our brightest and best young people are starving themselves slowly to death.

The best answer we seem to have come up with is 'magazines'. This says rather more about what society thinks goes on in the minds of teenage girls than it does about the cause of an epidemic that kills thousands of young people every year, and leaves countless more living half-existences with the best dreams of their single lives shrunk to the size of a dinner plate.

The most important thing to understand about eating

disorders is that starving, bingeing, purging and puking are not causes of distress. They are symptoms of it. The diseases are replete with contradictions, at once about denying hunger for food, for rest, for fun, for sex, for freedom while the sufferer starves for it all to the point of death.[3] Most curiously, these pathologies involve an intricate interplay of aggression and compliance. Eating disorders are what happens when youthful rebellion cannibalises itself.

And they're easier to conceal than most mental illnesses, especially in a visual culture where we've got used to images of extremely undernourished young people. Those that do not necessarily cause extreme weight loss, like bulimia nervosa and compulsive over-eating disorder, are easier still to keep secret – for a while. All of these illnesses take a frightening toll on the brain and body, both in the long and short term, as sufferers turn to all kinds of dangerous and grotesque methods to control their weight, from bloodletting, drug abuse and frantic over-exercise to vomiting until the cheeks swell and teeth rot from spewing stomach acid. It's not pretty. It's the ugly little open secret behind much of modern beauty culture, and the biggest secret is that it's no secret at all.

None of it is. So many young people are doing ritual violence to their own bodies. Diagnosis of eating disorders, chronic cutting and other, more arcane forms of self-injury has mushroomed over the past decade, especially among girls, young queers, anybody who's under extra pressure to fit in.

Maintaining order on the surface is important, even if underneath you are a seething wreck. We know that looking 'good', for a woman, involves sacrifice, weakness, hard work, illness, even death. The rituals of beauty and conformity demand hard labour, and if a woman happens to be born looking like a catwalk model, she is assumed to have cheated. The thin, miserable woman who sacrifices health, wealth and happiness to keeping her body in control has more social capital than the fat woman who has more important things on her mind.

Of all the female sins, hunger is the least forgivable; hunger for anything, for food, sex, power, education, even love. If we have desires, we are expected to conceal them, to control them, to keep ourselves in check. We are supposed to be objects of desire, not desiring beings. We do not need food: in many ways, we are food, trainable meat, lambs queuing up in line for gravy. We consume only what we are told to, from lipstick to life insurance, and only what will make us more consumable ourselves, the better to be chewed up and swallowed by a machine that wants our work, our money, our sexuality broken down into bite-sized chunks.

Men experience body policing too, of course, and there are real penalties for being overweight. The penalties, however, tend to be less existential; one can still, outside a very small range of professions, expect to be judged as a soul first and as a body second. Men's physicality is not assumed to be everything they have to contribute. Men who are overweight or ungroomed are rarely told that they will inevitably die alone. 'Beauty' for men, despite the best efforts of the cosmetics industry to persuade them otherwise, still involves little more than a shave, a slick of hair-gel and a clean T-shirt. 'Beauty' for women, by contrast, involves hours of pain and expense just to make it into the ballpark. Our bodies are the most important thing about us, and left to themselves, they will betray us, become fat and unmanageable: they must be controlled.

In Italy, there is a tradition called '*sciopero bianco*' – the white strike. In English-speaking countries, it is known as work-to-rule. Workers who are not permitted to strike fight their bosses by doing only what is required of them – to the letter. Nurses refuse to answer phones that ring at 17:01. Transport workers make safety checks so rigid that trains run hours behind schedule. Eating disorders and other forms of dangerous self-harm are to riots in the streets what a white strike is to a factory occupation: women, precarious workers, young people and others for whom the lassitudes of modern life routinely produce acute distress and for whom the stakes of social non-conformity are high, lash out by doing only what is required of them, to the point of extremity. Work hard, eat less, consume frantically; be thin and perfect and good, conform and comply, push yourself to the point of collapse. It is no accident that eating disorders are often associated with obsessive overwork and perfectionism at school, in the workplace or in the home. We followed all the rules, sufferers seem to be saying – now look what you made us do.

In school and at work, girls are easier to control than boys. We're more willing to memorise exam systems, more willing to take orders, more compliant,[4] and our reward is the perennial picture of ourselves or girls just like us on the front of the local paper jumping the air in low-cut tops, with good grades and pert arses, waving diplomas that will get us those coveted jobs in marketing.

Girls don't get to rebel in quite the same way that boys do. There's simply too much at stake. We know that we will not be indulged if we flame out, we have been taught to turn our anger inwards, to turn our rage inwards, to hurt ourselves rather than hurting others. According to the stereotype: where rebellious young men hurt other people, out-of-control young women hurt themselves, compulsively, dangerously. Eating disorders and self-harm, bingeing and purging and starving and cutting and burning, it all becomes a silent rhetoric of female distress. If you didn't grow up doing it yourself, you almost certainly knew someone who did. We experience this trauma on our bodies. It is a physical thing. It fucking hurts.

WORK IT, BABY

A great deal of what used to call itself 'new feminism' – before the word itself became too dicey for everyday women's magazines – used to devote itself to reassuring women and girls that they could be empowered, independent political women and still be beautiful. Or, at least, if they weren't beautiful, they could indulge in socially prescribed rituals of beauty. Articles and programmes like this are still based on the most prosaic, intimate type of questions: is it all right for empowered women to shave their legs? Can I be a feminist if I love to wear lipstick and twirly dresses? A lot of this nonsense is a response to the tired old stereotype of feminism as unbeautiful, and being unbeautiful – being ugly – is the very worst thing a woman can ever be.

That stereotype harks back to the Second-Wave feminists of the 1970s or 1980s, some of whom, yes, did wear trousers and go unshaved – but alongside Andrea Dworkin in her overalls, there was Gloria Steinem, whose classic bombshell looks allowed her to go undercover as a Playboy Bunny in Hugh Hefner's original club to write an excoriating exposé of how women were treated in that weird world; and there was Germaine Greer, with legs up to her earlobes posing half-naked on the cover of *Oz* as a new kind of sex symbol, all cheekbones and lean spread thighs and unashamed libido.

What the stereotype of the bra-burning, hairy-legged feminist is really supposed to suggest is that feminism, that politics itself, makes a woman ugly. That women's liberation is a threat to traditional ideas of femininity, of a woman's social role. Which, of course, it is, and always has been.

Women's fear of not being considered beautiful is well founded. Recent studies have proven what most of us have grown up knowing on a deep and painful level: that there is a cost, for every woman and girl, to departing from the norm of whatever her particular society considers 'beautiful'.[5] Women and girls who deviate from current beauty norms in physical appearance, weight, style, race or gender presentation face discrimination at work and quantifiable obstacles in terms of pay and promotion. These days the definition of 'beauty' has become narrowed, heightened and Westernised to the extent that it's almost impossible for any woman to attain in her everyday life, even if she is lucky enough to be born with a face and figure that fits her out for a modelling career. That, of course, is the point.

Participation in beauty culture, moreover, is not optional for a great number of women – particularly those of us who work precarious jobs where we are expected to devote more and more of our time, effort and energy to flirting, to service, to making customers feel warm and safe and snuggly. Right now, because I work from home, I'm sitting at my desk with my hair scraped back and my face bare, but if I'd turned up looking like this when I worked as a shopgirl in Camden market, I'd have been fired quicker than you can say 'professional double standard'. On the other hand, it's best not to be too pretty if you want to be taken seriously at work, or outside it.

Pretty girls get used to being treated like the enemy by other women. They are not the enemy. If you grow up weird-looking, it's easy to think of them as such. I used to be terrified of those to whom girlhood seemed to come naturally, the gorgeous, graceful creatures who flocked around the back of the school bus, flirting and texting. It took me years to understand that pretty privilege comes with its own set of problems. That pretty girls, too, have to put up with harassment and violence, with the constant pressure to pare down your flesh and desires, and with the feeling of being judged and dismissed.

A pretty young woman is a paradox: at once a figure of desire and disgust. Hers is the power that all women are supposed to want, the only power we're really allowed to have, the power to please and to play up to male sexual attention – and so it is vital that her power be put in its place. Anyone succeeding at the pretty girl game, however briefly, has to face the suspicion and hostility of other women as well as the worshipful contempt of men. She is assumed to be without consequence, to be intellectually void, to exist only for the pleasure of others; at best, she is a muse, a fascinating enigma. She is permitted hidden depths as long as they stay that way – hidden.

Girls and grown women are exhorted to be beautiful at all costs, to compete with other women, for love, for attention, for the few consolation prizes handed out to those who try hardest. Pretty girls and ugly girls are taught to fear one another: after all, if power is a product of 'erotic capital', there can be no solidarity between those who are competing for those consolation prizes. You can't win. If you choose to devote less of your time to grooming as a political statement, you're a 'hairy bra-burning feminist' and nobody has any obligation to listen to anything you have to say, but if you embrace conventional beauty standards, or appear to enjoy them for their own sake, you are presumed to be a shallow and manipulative slut.

It's interesting that 'ugly' is still the insult most commonly thrown at women to dismiss their power, to get them to shut up. Female politicians are called ugly and unfuckable by men who can't quite bring themselves to say directly that they don't deserve their power, that their primary purpose as women should be to please and arouse the opposite sex.[6] I've lost count of the times I've been told, on the Internet or in person, to 'shut up, ugly bitch,' when men – or, occasionally, women – were uncomfortable with something I was saying, or with the fact that I was a young woman saying anyting at all. At first I panicked, started turning up to talks and debates in my best slinky black clothes, in leather, in lipstick – but no amount of lipstick is ever going to make patriarchy comfortable with the words coming out of your mouth, if you've an ounce of courage, or ambition, or anger.

'Fat' is even more obvious. You're gross, you take up too much space, get out of my sight. Men who occupy positions of power, of course, are allowed to run to fat, to lose interest in their appearance, to turn up unshaved, bloated, haggard-looking after a night out networking: their places at the top table will still be reserved.

It's a system of judgement, of exclusion, that permeates social class. Naomi Wolf was right, in *The Beauty Myth*, to refer to 'Beauty Work' – the time, money and effort women have to put into 'maintaining' their appearance and cramming their physical selves into the narrow stereotype of conventional beauty standards – as a new 'third shift' of labour, alongside women's traditional 'second shift' of domestic and caring work. The irony, of course, is that when Wolf published *The Beauty Myth* at the age of twenty-nine, she was lambasted by men and women alike precisely because she was and remains conventionally beautiful.

At the same time, we're told that we're weak and stupid for caring. We're told that participation in traditional beauty culture is in some way capitulating, is fragility on a fundamental level, whether in ourselves or in others. Women who are expected to turn up for work in lipstick and high heels – recently a trade-union motion was overturned that would have prevented employers from forcing women to wear heels[7] – are often punished when they don't, but rarely taken seriously when they do.

The game is rigged. You can't win, because nobody wins. If you don't diet, blow-out your hair, spend your spare cash on beauty treatments and fashionable clothes, you're considered inferior, letting down professional standards – but if you do, you're an idiot bimbo. Incidentally, here's the answer to the weary question of whether leg-shaving and bikini-waxing prevents you from being a feminist. Of course it doesn't. It doesn't, and we need to stop writing articles about it.

Of course you can remove the hair on your legs, straighten the hair on your head, wear high heels and pink glitter and play with make-up. I do some or most of those things whenever I go out in girl-drag.[8] Feminism isn't about telling women what not to wear. Nor is it about saying that every wardrobe choice you make is unproblematic, let alone likely to lead to sexual revolution. The fall of patriarchy is unlikely to begin or end with one woman's decision to wear fishnets or grow out her armpit hair, so relax. Make informed choices, play with gender, wear what you want. Feminism is far more than a big-girls' squabble over the dressing-up box, and there are more important things to do.

Gender determines the shape of our fantasies. Good little boys are supposed to dream about changing the world, but good little girls are supposed to dream about changing ourselves. From the first time we open a book of fairy tales, we learn that beauty is destiny, and when we grow up, we're told that this destiny is ours to command. If we can consume wisely enough to be beautiful and fashionable, we can transform everything about ourselves.

When beauty becomes mandatory, it ceases to be about fun, about play. Dressing up, playing with gender roles, doing your braids badly in the mirror, and eating half your mother's lipstick in an attempt to get it on your face – do you remember when that used to be fun? And do you remember when the fun stopped? Like any game, the woman game stops being fun when you start playing to win, especially if you've got no choice: win or be ridiculed, win or become invisible, dismissed, disturbed. When I was in the hospital, the markers of psychological health among young women were long hair, pretty dresses, shopping and make-up. The middle-aged, ponderously paunched male psychiatrists who ran the ward were absolutely in agreement on that point – to become healthy we had to 'embrace our feminity'. The latest right-on theories about eating disorders posit the diseases as a method that young women use to escape the stresses of modern femininity.[9] Anorexia nervosa, the logic goes, suspends the traumatic process of becoming a woman, because when you stop eating, when you cut down from 600 to 400 to 200 calories per day, your periods stop, your tits and hips and wobbly bits disappear, and you return to an artificial prepubescent state, complete with mood swings, weird musical obsessions, and the overpowering impulse to shoplift scrunchies from the cornershop. The reason young women and increasing numbers of young men behave like this, the logic goes, is because they're scared and angry about the gender roles that they are being forced into. The notion that they might have damn good reasons for being scared and angry has not yet occurred to the psychiatric profession.

BREAKING THE GAME

In the school ward for the re-education of wilful non-eaters, sex talk was not permitted. Swearing was not permitted. In mandatory art-therapy sessions, me and two other girls drew huge, hairy cocks and cunts and crude sex scenes on the sheets of paper provided for us to express our feelings, and were called to explain why we were being so stubborn and not progressing as planned. In the line to get weighed in the morning we'd whisper *minge* and *fanny* to each other to see how loud we could get before the nurses shut us up. We had to behave. We had to be good girls, if we ever wanted to leave.

In that place, if you wanted to go out the front door and not in a box, you had to play by their rules. You had to smile and eat your meals. You had to be a good girl. That meant no more trousers, no more going out with short hair and no make-up, finding a boyfriend as soon as possible, and learning to style your hair and do your eyeliner. It meant buying different dresses for different occasions, fitting yourself out to have men look at you with lust, learning manners, learning to dip your head and say 'Please' and 'Thank you' and 'No cake for me, I've been naughty enough this week.'

That was proper femininity, straight femininity, femininity as control, as a great unqueering. It was the makeover to end all makeovers, and we helped each other, dressing each other up in clothes and make-up like cracked-out Barbie dolls, even me – especially me, because I'd come in wearing short hair and trousers and talking about kissing girls, so I had the most to learn about what a woman really was. We all played the game with one another, especially when one of us was allowed to leave the ward, dressing and painting and polishing her nails and doing her hair, sending her off into the world a healthy, normal woman, not the damaged, fragile person who had walked or been wheeled in months before with her heart unskinned.

Make yourself up. Make yourself new. Play the woman game, and play it better than your friends. You're all surface, after all, and you'd better make the surface interesting, modern and new, because what's underneath is just another woman with her petty problems and boring emotions. Makeover shows, from *America's Next Top Model* to *The Swan* to *Snog, Marry, Avoid* and their endless iterations have been some of the most long-running and popular television franchises of the past two decades. This is no accident.

For modern women in this anxious age, the makeover is a ritual of health and devotion and social conformity. It's the central transfigurative myth of modern femininity, and it's lucrative. Playing the woman game, the game of artifice and self-annihilation, is serious business. A recent survey by shopping channel QVC claimed that the average British woman spends £2,055 per year, or 11 per cent of the median full-time female salary, on maintaining and updating the way she looks. Men, by contrast, spend just 4 per cent of their salary on their appearance, most of which goes on shaving and the gym.[10] Glossy women's magazines are manuals of self-transformation: change your body for summer, change your wardrobe for winter, learn to look at the world through smoky eyes, sparkly eyes or natural eyes, which require just as much paint as the rest. Cosmetic-surgery companies plaster public transport with promises to deliver not just physical changes, but emotional ones like 'confidence'. Fashion editorials advise us to spend money we don't have on skirt suits and handbags as 'investment pieces'; you're not supposed to dress and style your body simply to please yourself but with one eye on your financial future.

That skirt suit really is an 'investment' in a one-woman business whose product is you, only glossier. This is what power, health and success means to the modern, emancipated woman: terminal exhaustion and a wardrobe full of expensive disguises.

Femininity, docility and prettiness, by which we mean the lifelong effort to look as much like an even-featured, underweight Caucasian girl in her early twenties as possible, are the entry tickets to a wide variety of jobs in which a few will make it big and most won't make it out.

It turns out that they lied to us. The magazines lied, the movies lied, our mothers lied. Being a beautiful girl does not make everything better. It does not, in fact, make anything very much better at all, it just gives you a different set of problems, as anyone who became briefly pretty after school was over, like I did, knows for sure. Little girls learn that being beautiful is the only sure route to love, liberty and happiness, and if they are born beautiful, it doesn't matter if they're born poor. The mythology of beauty isn't very different from the fairy tale of the beautiful girl who grows up to marry the prince in centuries of children's stories, except that today the prince is an optional extra, part of the package of fame and money and adoration rather than the only ticket to all those things we're supposed to crave. Of the endless lists of the richest, most powerful and most admired women in the world, most of them still got there by being beautiful, by marrying a powerful man, or both. Hillary Rodham Clinton may have been Secretary of State, but she is still judged for her fuckability and ability to rock a pantsuit. The sole regular exception is the Queen of England, in whose case it doesn't matter how much Botox you haven't had if you own half of Antarctica and look scary on a stamp.

Beauty is about class, and it always has been. Centuries ago, the aspirational 'beauties' of the age were the trophy wives and daughters of wealthy men who could afford to keep 'their' women idle and dress them in impractical finery; today you are expected to look as if you're rich enough not to have to work if you want to have a career. The extra time, money and energy women spend on their appearance increases every year, and is surprisingly resistant to the economic downturn:[11] it's almost as if someone had been telling us from before we had language that beauty was necessary for survival. What's the first thing you say to a baby with a bow in her hair? Who's a pretty girl?

Women and girls grow up learning that whatever we do with our three score and ten years on this planet, however brave and smart and accomplished we are, however many millions we earn or lives we save, none of it matters if we are not beautiful. In fact, we need to be beautiful if we want to be loved, powerful and successful; those few women who get to be in the public eye without the measurements of a teenage Siberian gymnast, from television academics to Secretaries of State, are mercilessly ridiculed and attacked for their appearance in newspapers and magazines, on television and online, judged on their attractiveness to men. We are reminded that we must be a hot babe – an ideal subject – or be ridiculed.

Little girls learn all this because it's important that they don't question what they're supposed to want, and who they're supposed to want to be, to be with and to bring into the world. Don't have kids too early, that's what poor girls do, but don't forget to have them as soon as you can afford the nanny. And if you are the nanny? Well, just wear a cute dress and smile and hope you get home in time to finish your schoolwork or put your own kids to bed. What, are you tired even thinking about it? Does something inside you shiver at the thought of forty years of ruthless conformity, or time and expense and hunger and self-hate and sacrifice, all for the chance, only the chance of being safe and loved? Do you worry that you won't ever be enough?

Well, you're right to worry. Of course you won't be enough. You can never be enough. Only perfect, beautiful women deserve love and fulfilment; you, on the other hand, are weak, ugly, lazy and fat. If you aren't happy, it's your own fault. You should have worked harder. You should have eaten less and saved up for that nose job. You should have been smarter, thinner, nicer, taller, whiter, prettier, more in control of your ghastly self. Worrying about not having enough is still coded masculine, although poverty is still, overwhelmingly, a feminine experience.[12] Men want objects; women are objects. Men's first desire is to have enough things and do enough things; women simply want to be enough. Men want; women are wanted. And for women, to be undesirable is still a real existential threat. Women who are not stereotypically attractive, young and able-bodied often speak of feeling 'invisible' – as if they don't exist.

UNSPEAKABLE HUNGER

The more powerful women become, the more we are taught that our bodies are unacceptable. Many of the most influential women in the world, from pop stars to media tycoons, have faced public battles with their weight that the tabloid press is only too happy to catalogue and exaggerate. Others, particularly politicians, have faced popular ridicule for the apparently scandalous surfeit of flesh on their perfectly normal-sized bellies and bottoms.

A report published in a recent issue of the *Journal of Applied Psychology*[13] revealed that the pay and influence of test groups of women in America and Germany consistently rose as their weight dropped below the healthy average, even when controlling for other factors that affect both weight and pay. By contrast, weight gain was an indicator of financial success for males up to the point of extreme obesity, when men too begin to pay a professional penalty.

Causality is always difficult to establish. Even with a rigorous study, it is impossible to say conclusively whether the women lost weight because their salaries rose, or whether their salaries rose because they lost weight. One thing's for certain, though: in Europe and America, fear of female flesh is fear of female power, and Western society's stage-managed loathing for women's normal-sized bodies is deeply political. Even at the very top of the food chain, women's hunger must be contained at all costs if the present state of things is to continue. Thus far, and no further, and it'd be nice if you had a run around with the hoover while you're up there.

This study is hard evidence of what most women with a

scrap of personal and professional ambition have understood instinctively for the majority of our lives: that our success in life and at work is likely to be in inverse proportion to the number of spare inches of meat on our bones, and that our normal, healthy bodies are not wanted in positions of power. After a century of feminism, a few women are now permitted to hold authoritative roles in business, media and politics – but only so long as we take up as little physical space as possible. If there's one type of woman the media can't stand, it's a political heavyweight.

That's nothing, however, when compared to the utter horror society reserves for larger women who are also poor. The fact that in Western countries, where quantity of food access isn't as problematic as quality, being overweight is as likely to be a symptom of poverty and malnutrition has only cemented the barely concealed disgust of the cultural right for working-class women who take up too much space.

From the boardrooms to the streets, women's anxiety to keep our body mass as low as possible is based on legitimate fears that we will be punished if we attempt fully to enter patriarchal space. No wonder so many of us are starving.

The best way to stop girls achieving anything is to force them to achieve everything. Where once feminists complained of women's 'second shift' of housework and childcare outside the workplace, the obligation to be highly achieving now infects every part of life: we must be academically successful, socially graceful, physically attractive, sexually alluring but not too 'slutty', talented but not 'pushy'.

One of the first things girls learn is our own powerlessness.

I mean our physical powerlessness: the idea, true or untrue, that boys are stronger and fitter, and always will be. Some months before the Olympic games, *Grazia* magazine published an editorial detailing the exercises athletics champions do to train their bodies – all posed by fashion models in couture gowns arranged to give the impression they were barely able to lift the props in their hands.[14] Strong-bodied women do not impress advertisers, that's why the pictures of the actual athletes were in miniature at the bottom of the page. Women aren't allowed to look like they might be able to fuck you up. The only thing we are allowed to punch is a pillow, preferably in our underwear with a camera flashing, and pillow-fighting patriarchy isn't even going to slow it down.

The battles of the young girl under late capitalism are the battles of the age, for dignity and gender and identity. The young girl, whose abjectness is part of her charm, is supposed to know better than anyone else that her misery is her own fault. She senses that she is fashioning herself into a commodity, meat for the cubicle moulded in plastic, but when her soul rebels she assumes the problem is that she isn't a good-enough commodity, and works harder to shave off her strange and painful edges.

So, she works. All girls work. We spend money we don't have in order to express the inner self we wish we had, the good and beautiful creature who deserves to be saved. We all know, as every working person who watches films knows, that our true self is rich and pretty and popular, and if we only put on the right clothes and learn to walk the walk, that's who we will become. Fulfilment is an individual, and not a structural matter, and it is mediated by rigid conformity, which is of course the best way of being an individual, just like everybody else.

Perhaps the cruellest trick played on my mother's generation was the way they were duped into believing that the right to work in every low-paid, back-breaking job men do was the only and ultimate achievement of the women's movement. Yes, in most Western countries, women now have the legal right to be paid equally for any job a man can do, although they have to get the job first.

In practice, however, women are not working at the top of the pay and employment scale in large numbers. We are instead over-represented in low-paid, underpaid and unpaid work, just as we always have been, in domestic and care-sector work and other professions that remain at the bottom of the social heap in terms of pay and social status precisely because that work is traditionally done by women. The idea that this represents the end point of feminist progress needs to be done away with, and quickly.

PERFECT GIRLS

Society understands that young girls are fucked up. That's part of their charm. They're not just objects, they are abject, terminally unable to cope with the exigencies of adult life, of the bewildering array of life choices modern society offers us, from vaginal butchery to jobs in the service sector. Western womankind is collectively imagined as a toddler let loose in a candy store, so overwhelmed by the range of options that it has an ungrateful tantrum and is sick on the floor. And fucked-up young girls grow up to be miserable women:

study after vaunted study tells us that women and girls are as miserable as they have ever been, overworked, exhausted, taking prescription medication in three times the numbers of men.[15] The front pages of celebrity magazines shriek out a chorus of successful women on the verge of mental and physical collapse: this star is starving herself, this one is depressed, this one is drinking herself into a nightly stupor until her children are confiscated. It's a myth that pleases the powerful. Women have all this equality and opportunity now, but we can't handle it. Maybe we weren't meant to have it in the first place.

It's hard growing up; it's easier to grow sideways, to veer off from becoming a person and just be a girl instead. After all, it's what your family want. They want you to be pretty and pleasing and no trouble at all. It's not because they hate you and want to keep you down, but because they want what's best for you, and objective observation of the world suggests that girls who are ugly and troublesome tend to have problems, or become problems, and nobody wants you to be a problem. It's what your boyfriend wants. He has not been raised to expect a relationship with a real human being, but a sidekick, a helpmeet, a wank-fantasy made only-just flesh. And it's what your boss wants. He – or she – wants you to play the game. Be a good girl. Smile and make people feel comfortable; accept low pay, long hours, the occasional grope in the corridor, compete with other young women to be the prettiest and most compliant, the hardest-working, the girl everyone loves. Just don't ever aspire to be more than that.

Being a girl, being That Girl, is easy if you're white and

averagely pretty. There's no trick to it. You don't even have to totally excise the parts of your personality that don't fit, the parts that are smart and difficult and loud and angry and ambitious and masculine and mature. You just dial those parts down until they become background noise, dial them down and down until the male ear can't pick up their frequency and pretty soon you won't even be able to hear them inside your own head. Tune them out and swallow them down like the hot meals you can't eat any more because That Girl must stay slim and fragile if she wants to be beautiful and loved. And you do want to be beautiful and loved.

Most of all, it is tiring. It is tiring to be constantly scrambling for the moving edge of perfection, denying yourself rest, forgoing sleep, fighting to be better at everything. Perfect girls know that they must constantly improve. Perfect girls don't sit on the sofa eating biscuits, even when their very favourite show is on. Perfect girls are always working: when they are not at school or on the clock they are working out, and when they aren't working out they are volunteering, shopping, or running a social life like a frantic start-up. The cruellest lie they were told as girls was 'it's what's on the inside that counts'. It is not what's on the inside that counts. Perfect girls don't get a day off. Characters who are largely fictional rarely do.

Here are a few more things perfect girls don't get.

They don't get to eat a slice of birthday cake without considering its fat content. They don't get to put themselves first, or even second. They don't get to make mistakes, which means they never really get to grow up, which means they can only ever get old, which is a fearful thing for girl-children. They don't get to go out looking sloppy and roll down a hill in the park just for the hell of it.

And if they fail, if they fuck up, they don't get forgiven.

This is why girls are so much more employable than young men in all the shitty, less-than-subsistence-level service jobs they're trying to cram young people into across Europe and America. Girls are better at pleasing other people and plastering on the pretty grin even when we're screaming inside. That's what being a girl is.

Girls are better at this sort of labour, often called 'emotional labour', not because there's anything in the meat and matter of our living cells that makes us naturally better but because we're trained to it from birth. Trained to make other people feel good. Trained to serve the coffee, fill in the forms, organise the parties and wipe the table afterwards. Trained to be feisty, if we must, but not strong. To be bubbly, not funny. You must at no stage appear to have a body that functions in a normal human way, that pisses and shits and sweats and farts and falters. Decorate the prison of your body. Make yourself useful. Shut up and smile.

THE PRIVILEGE OF REBELLION

The Beat Poet Gregory Corso, when asked why there were so few women among the half-mad, celebrated, drug-taking, sexually experimental Beat Writers of the 1950s, said: 'There were women, they were there, I knew them, their families put them in institutions, they were given electric shock. In the '50s if you were male you could be a rebel, but if you were female your families had you locked up. There were cases, I knew them, someday someone will write about them.'[16]

Sanity is still socially determined, just as rebellion is still riskier if you're a girl. It is as much about how you behave as it is about how you feel. You can be collapsing on the inside but as long as you can put your make-up on and smile for your boss or teacher, you're okay. Conversely, you can be a functioning weird kid who just happens to have non-standard priorities and that shit can get you shoved on behavioural medication, deemed anti-social or locked up, depending on where you live.

Sanity is socially determined, and the bar of normality for women and girls is dauntingly high, a task requiring training. None of this means that distress is not real. On the contrary: it is often the effort to appear normal, the staggering amount of existential and personal work it requires to be the sort of perfect girl we're all told gets to be loved and happy, that creates the distress in the first place.

You can spend your whole life being a perfect girl, never growing up, just gradually, resentfully, growing old. Choosing to grow up is painful, after all, especially if you've picked up on the fact that becoming a grown woman is the worst possible thing a girl can do. Don't get older. Don't talk back. Don't think too hard, it puts ugly lines in your forehead. Stay pretty and perfect and pliant and silent. You can have whatever you want as long as you don't ask for too much: let the magazines and adverts decide what you really desire, defer to your boyfriend and your teachers and your boss. We know what you want better than you do, and if you have a problem with that, we have a pill for what ails you.

There are treatments for everything wrong with you: for your body that thickens and ages, your sex organs that leak and bleed and show outside your body, your heart that tires and cries out in fear. We can preserve you as the perfect girl, the perfect consumer, the perfect worker, all surface with a few subtle slits for easy penetration. Ageing can and must be fought with creams and pills and injections and knives; all evidence of your body having been lived in can be starved or burnt away.

The perfect girl is a blank slate, with just enough personality to make her interesting enough to take to bed. Personality, for the perfect girl as imagined by male writers and employers and lovers generations since, is an accessory, not a fact of agency. Personality for the perfect girl is a well-chosen accessory, worn discreetly to emphasise her most appealing features.

The perfect girl has little interest in the wider world. She has no interiority either, except the minimum necessary to hold a man's interest between chance meeting and the bedroom floor. She is neither an internal nor an external creature; instead, the perfect girl is all surface. The surface is all that matters.

Of course, nobody is really a perfect girl.

Seventeen and curled like a comma under that hospital bed, like an unfinished sentence, stuttering. The freakish hall light that never gets turned off casts a cage-shadow on the snot-coloured carpet. I shake. I am coming off everything. I still refuse to eat, but my resistance is wearing away. I am coming down from the precipice where it was all clear and precise and lined with the promise of death like the school blazer hanging off my skeleton. This morning I told a doctor trying to force me to gulp down a disgusting protein drink that I didn't want it, and she asked me, what do you want?

The answer snags in my teeth like a sob – I don't want anything. I don't want anything. I don't want food water air attention a new world order. I don't want fifty years of never being enough, doing enough, working enough. I don't even want you to leave me alone to die. Stay there and watch if you fucking want, I don't care.

I don't want anything. I whisper it into my hands, and then louder, over and over, for hours, until the long-suffering night-nurse, who is used to this sort of crazy shit, finally comes in and tells me to shut up and go to sleep. She appreciates that I don't want anything, but she wants a quiet night, please.

I am something of an anomaly on the ward. I arrived with close-cropped hair, soaked in hair dye and Riot Grrl Rock, dressed as a boy, obviously queer. It's only later that I will learn that between a quarter and a half of young people hospitalised with eating disorders are gay or genderqueer. The young women who meet me here look like broken dress-up dolls, all of us poured from the same weird, emaciated mould, barely able to stand upright, the same violent cut marks scored like barcodes in the secret places on our skin.

There's Ballerina Barbie, starved too small for adult leotards, huddling in the corner; there's Babydoll Barbie and Hip-Hop Barbie and Cheerleader Barbie and even Devout Muslim Barbie, who turns up a week after I do in full hijab, which she throws off as soon as her parents leave to spend the rest of her inpatient stay chain-smoking on the front steps in a hot-pink tracksuit. Me, I suppose I'd be Punk-Dyke Barbie, 2004's least popular Barbie, and my MO is mistrust. The other girls on the ward look like every kind of girl I'd grown up afraid of. I expect every one of them to pour orange juice in my backpack when I'm not looking. It's bad enough being on a locked ward, but now I have to be locked up with a bunch of frivolous fashion kids? Clearly, these girls have starved themselves to the point of collapse simply because they want to look pretty; I, meanwhile, have perfectly rational, intellectual reasons for doing exactly the same. We will never be friends. We have nothing in common.

This point of view lasts almost exactly eighteen hours, until the first scheduled late-night feeding time, when we all huddle together on cheap hospital sofas trying to push two puny biscuits into our faces, feeling boiled in our skin. I stare at the television and will myself not to cry. And Cheerleader Barbie, who is ten years older than me and has her own story, shunts close and puts a bony arm around my shoulders.

'It's all right,' she tells me. 'You can do it.'

I allow myself to be held. I pick up the biscuit. And something changes.

Over the weeks and months of confinement, these girls will become my greatest friends. I will learn at seventeen what it takes some people decades to accept: that pretty girls who play to patriarchy and ugly girls who never got asked to a school dance suffer just the same. That the same trick is being played on all of us. There's no way to play the perfect-girl game and win. I know that. We all know that. And with that knowledge comes anger. Anger that we tried to starve down and burn off and bleed out.

Cindy cuts like any girl who has been hurt by the people who were supposed to love her. Because she acts out, because she slashes her arms in the corridor and screams, because she steals make-up and jewellery from the shops and vomits after mealtimes, the nurses and doctors don't quite believe her when she tells us that her dad molested her. That she doesn't want to be left alone with him if he comes to visit. That her mother and teachers knew it was going on and did nothing. She is an angry Asian girl with an accent: she ought to respect her parents, she's clearly crazy and shouldn't be taken seriously. Drugs and therapy might help her; nobody talks about justice.

Cutting calms Cindy down and upsets everyone else, which to my mind is an improvement on silently suffocating in her pain and rage, although I'd rather she didn't break my CDs to do it. I'd rather she didn't do it at all. I'd rather she didn't need to. I'd rather take Cindy in my arms and rock her until she forgets every bad thing that has ever been done to her.

Half the girls in the ward are cutters, which is why sharp cutlery and smashable crockery are kept out of reach. The body must be punished, and locked up indoors, this is the last, best way to do so. There are words that can't be spoken, and get scored into the skin. You think I'm all right, but I'm not. When you grow up to find yourself trapped in a body that seems to invite violence, a body that seems to be all you're good for, a body that is suddenly and forever the most important thing about you, there is a grim logic to the attempt to cut your way out of it. To discipline it and bring it under your control. The body that hurts, and hungers, and ceaselessly wants things. The body that betrays you.

Being a good girl can kill you. In her 'Letters to L', M. Sandovsky writes that 'The problem for women is not just uncovering what is political in the personal and personal in the political. It is finding a way to live inside of a contradiction.'[17] We grew up being told that the world was ours for the taking as long as we worked hard, flashed a bit of tit and kept smiling. We realised we were being lied to only just in time for some of us to catch ourselves before we slipped away.

You reach a point where you have to decide what you will sacrifice to survive. It was years ago now, and enough has happened to me since that I've forgotten when it was that I decided to give living a shot, just as an experiment, to see if I could. Maybe it was after the long, howling night of not wanting everything, levering myself out from under the bed, blinking in the hall lights, shuffling to the small medical kitchen to eat toast for the first time without fighting. I just remember the crisp, buttery bread, and the fear that if I let my hunger loose I'd never stop eating, I'd eat and eat until I was the size of a monster truck and keep eating until I'd swallowed the world. A young girl's hunger is a fearful thing.

Or maybe it was months later, leaving hospital for the first time in a new dress and lipstick I'd put on to convince the ward nurse that I was finally a healthy girl, ready to live a healthy life, painting on an expression the way women learn to do when we have to convince the world we're happy. Waving bye-bye to the friends I'd made there from the window of a taxi taking me hell-knows-where, though not home. I knew only that I would not be going home ever again. I was going to get out of this place and continue my education, I would travel the world and get drunk in strange bars and fuck a lot of boys and kiss a lot of girls, I would live in Berlin and New York and cross oceans at night with only a satchel, a passport and a laptop. I would dance all night in bare feet and read a lot of books, and some day I'd write books, too.

Being a good girl, a perfect girl, can kill you fast, or it can kill you slow, flattening everything precious inside you, the best dreams of your one life, into drab homogeneity. At seventeen I decided to make a stab at a different kind of life, and it was scary, and too much, and it still is, but so is staying at home with a painted-on smile. I see women making that choice every day, in their teens and twenties and sixties and seventies, and in this brave new world where empowerment means expensive shoes and the choice to bend over for your boss, it's the only choice that really matters. Those who make it get called selfish bitches, freaks and sluts and cunts and whores, and sometimes we get called rebels and degenerates and troublemakers, and sometimes we are known to the police. We're the ones who laugh too loud and talk too much and reach too high and work for ourselves and see a new world just out of reach, at the edge of language, struggling to be spoken. And sometimes, in the narrow hours of the night, we call ourselves feminists.

2

Lost Boys

Patriarchal masculinity estranges men from their selfhood.
bell hooks, *All About Love*

Some of my best friends are straight white men. It's not their fault. They didn't ask for that particular privilege, because that's not how privilege works, and now they don't know what to do with it except pretend it isn't there. But if we want to understand gender, power and desire, we must talk about men.

Where is the power today's young men were promised? Over five years of financial catastrophe and youth unemployment, I have watched countless young men, some of them very close to me, quietly drowning. The recession hasn't been Disneyland for young women either, but we have proved, in some ways, more emotionally robust. Fewer of us were raised to expect dignified work or financial security as an identity-forming part of our futures, and most of us were trained to accommodate exploitation on and off the job, which is exactly what today's employers are looking for.

Feminism has never just been about liberating women from men, but about freeing every human being from the straitjacket of gender oppression. For the first time, men and boys as a whole are starting to realise how profoundly messed up masculinity is – and to ask how they might make it different.

Masculinity matters to politics, and men matter to feminism. Their violence matters, and so does their fear – collective, articulated terror that, as society seems increasingly stacked against individual men, terror that they might lose even the scraps of privilege propping up their collapsing self-worth. How should men and boys behave, when male privilege doesn't necessarily mean power?

Rock and roll can't save you any more. I learn that first coming home from the shops one day in 2009, when I nearly step on the wreckage of a blue guitar, its guts spilt on the hall carpet in a tangle of wire and shattered wood. The blue guitar is destroyed, utterly beyond repair, its back broken, its tongue ripped out. The air tastes of weed smoke and sadness.

In the kitchen, my best friend is bleeding from his face.

I put my bags down and the kettle on, because that's what you do at times like this. My best friend sits quite still on the one kitchen chair that still has all four legs and dabs at his face with a bit of soggy toilet paper, and tea is hot and sweet and good for shock. Another bad day at the Jobcentre.

'He smashed up his guitar with his head,' says our housemate, when he goes into the bathroom. 'He came home from that interview and then he started headbutting it and screaming that he was no good for anything.'

We've been friends for years, since the first time we met in the hall at college, before the crash, before all the bullshit, back when we were nineteen and going to save the world with art. Just bookish bullied middle-class suburban kids who wanted to stay up late writing and getting into trouble. We scraped through our degrees and scarfed down our days like cheap cornershop wine, intoxicating in its guilty predictability. Four good summers.

And then college was over and the recession hit and the music got darker and angrier and failed to pay the rent. And the only interview an arts graduate with no family money for an internship could get was for a job as an interviewer at the Jobcentre, and the future was opening up like a great dark mouth.

Too many nights in the emergency room. Not enough money to go to the pub. It turns out that love wasn't enough, and working hard wasn't enough, and rock and roll can't save you. Maybe it could, once. Those days disappeared with punk and welfare.

We fill in the forms begging the council for money to buy food, money that only comes after a month of toast on Turnpike Lane, and write angry political lyrics and upload them to the band site, and it does no good. This Machine Does Not Kill Fascists. We personally tested this by playing loud Nick Cave covers all night to upset the member of the British National Party who lived down the road, and he appeared to remain in rude health.

And then one day, the music just stopped.

More than anything I wanted to save my best friend from despair and inspire him to great works. I did a horrible job of it, and I ended up hurting and exhausting us both in the process. These days, when I see friends, lovers and partners of sad, lost young men doing it anyway, and I want to shake them hard by the shoulders and shout that you can't save them. At least not like that.

Life gets a lot simpler when you realise you can't save them. The lost boys, and the young people determined not to be found because they're worried about what you might find. You can't save them with your love, no matter how much of it you have. You can wring out your heart on the floor in front of them but it won't ever be enough to float them off to a better world. And I know you would, if you could. That's what love means, at least when you're young and broke and don't know better.

This generation is lousy with lost boys, and loving one of them means hollowing yourself out to make a space for them to crawl inside. So you do that, because that's what girls are supposed to do, and because it's so good to be needed. Just for a little while. Just until your boyfriend gets a job and your best friend stops trying to kill himself.

I learned the truth at twenty-two: you can't save the world one man at a time.

Watching these young men growing up into a very different world from the one they were promised, my first reaction has always been sympathy. It's surprisingly easy to sympathise. For two reasons.

Firstly because so much of our culture is set up to make it easy to sympathise with white, middle-class cis men, who get to be the heroes of almost every story. We are not encouraged to understand the suffering of women or the very poor in quite the same way. They are unlike us, even when they are us, these people shut out by prejudice and austerity and fighting for a voice at the edge of what is considered relevant discourse.

And secondly because the disappointment of young white guys is so very raw. They grew up expecting the whole world in a lunchbox, and now, too often for comfort, they can't even get themselves a sandwich. At least, that's what I pick up from the number of anonymous men on the Internet who seem so desperate for me to make them one.[1]

When you were anticipating power and ease, not getting it stings like a slap.

There has been much discussion of the cohort of young adults born around the fall of the Berlin Wall as a 'lost generation', their dreams of prosperity dashed by the global recession. But let us be clear. When we talk about the young people who became adults after the dream of perpetual neoliberal expansion had died, after the jobs had disappeared and the funding had run out and the police had come out of the inner cities on to the main streets of every capital city to smash heads, when we talk about kids who suffered and imploded under the pressure of unmet expectations, we're talking about men. When we talk about the 'lost generation', we are talking about men.

It is men's dashed dreams that seem to matter most. And it is men's resentful rage that makes their frustration fearful.

NO MORE NEVER NEVER LAND

For people who have grown up relying on privilege without even having to think about it too much, the sudden loss of that privilege hits you like a fist to the stomach on a sunny day – it's the punch you weren't expecting. Suddenly all of the things you thought were just going to happen to you when you reached a certain age, along with pubic hair and tax returns, don't; it turns out that being part of the dominant half of the human race, being sexually and socially superior to women, being first in line for jobs and promotion, being taken seriously at work and at home, having your ideas listened to on their own merit precisely because you are a man – none of that is encoded. It is not your genetic inheritance. And it can be taken away.

How are men supposed to cope with this loss of power in a society that still insists that the only way to be a man is to grab as much power as possible, to be rich, to be capable of extreme violence, to dominate other men physically and to dominate women sexually and emotionally? The received wisdom is that they're not supposed to cope. Without power over others, particularly over women, men are supposed to crumble, to lash out, to collapse in an extravagant welter of identity implosion that leaves a suspicious mess on the carpet. If this is really the case, then men must be fragile creatures indeed.

Books and studies like Hanna Rosin's *The End of Men* have concluded that men's loss of power is women's gain. As we will see, the opposite is the case.

THIS IS GOING TO HURT

The great obstacle to women's progress is not men's hate, but their fear. The 'Men's Rights Activists' who organise to drown out and silence women on the Internet are usually fearful, lonely creatures who are desperate to speak about gender, but only able to do so as a way of shutting women down. That expression of fear comes from a profoundly childish place, a posture which is as fascistic in its policing of gender roles as a playground bully, and which uses words like 'Feminazi' with apparent seriousness. Because fighting for equality was what the Nazis were really known for.

It is as if by talking about the hurt women experience, often because we are women, we are somehow preventing men from speaking about the painful pressures of masculinity. Interestingly, for many men, the only time they do feel able to talk about their own suffering is when they are trying to stop women talking about theirs. In every other context, men and boys are discouraged from talking about their pain. Thinking in a new way about sex, gender and power – call it feminism or 'masculism' or whatever the hell you like as long as you do it – can help men to process that pain. But it's far easier just to blame women.

As more and more women and girls and a growing number of male allies start speaking out against sexism and injustice, a curious thing is happening: some people are complaining that speaking about prejudice is itself prejudice.

Increasingly, before we talk about misogyny, women are asked to modify our language so that we don't hurt men's feelings. Don't say 'men oppress women' – that's sexism, just as bad as any sexism women ever have to handle, and possibly worse. Instead, say 'some men oppress women'. Whatever you do, don't generalise. That's something men do. Not all men, of course, just some men.

This type of semantic squabbling is a very effective way of getting women to shut up. After all, most of us grew up learning that being a good girl was all about putting other people's feelings ahead of our own. We aren't supposed to say what we think if there's a chance it might upset somebody else, or worse, make them angry. I see this used as a silencing technique across the social justice movements with which I am associated: black people are asked to consider the feelings of white people before they speak about their own experience; gay and transsexual people are asked not to be too angry because it makes straight people feel uncomfortable. And so we start to stifle our speech with apologies, caveats and soothing sounds. We reassure our friends and loved ones that of course, you're not one of those dudes. You're not one of those racists, or those homophobes, or those men who hate women.

What we don't say is: of course not all men hate women. But culture hates women, and men who grow up in a sexist culture have a tendency to do and say sexist things, often without meaning to. We aren't judging you for who you are, but that doesn't mean we're not asking you to change your behaviour. What you feel about women in your heart is of less immediate importance than how you treat them on a daily basis. You can be the gentlest, sweetest man in the world and still benefit from sexism, still hesitate to speak up when you see women hurt and discriminated against. That's how oppression works. Thousands of otherwise decent people are persuaded to go along with an unfair system because changing it seems like too much bother. The appropriate response when somebody demands a change in that unfair system is to listen, rather than turn away or yell, as a child might, that it's not your fault. Of course it isn't your fault. I'm sure you're lovely. That doesn't mean you don't have a responsibility to do something about it.

Society tends to discourage us from thinking structurally. Pondering upsetting things like poverty, racism and sexism as parts of a larger architecture of violence does not come easy in a culture that prefers that we all see ourselves as free-acting individuals. But the body politic is riddled with bigotry like an infection: you can't see it or touch it until it breaks out on the skin. But it's there, under the surface, bursting and suppurating in individual wounds that suggest something else is going on under the surface. Your friend is raped by another friend at a party; your colleague has to leave work because she can't afford full-time childcare; your daughter comes home sobbing that she feels fat and refuses to eat dinner. It's simpler and less scary to imagine all of these things as individual, unrelated experiences, rather than part of a structure of sexism that infects everyone. Even you.

Dull gender stereotypes about multitasking aside, it's relatively easy to hold more than one idea in the human brain at a time. It's a large, complex organ, the brain, about the size and weight of a cauliflower, and it has room for many seasons' worth of trashy TV plotlines and the phone number of the ex-lover you really shouldn't be calling after six shots of vodka. If it couldn't handle big structural ideas at the same time as smaller personal ones, we would never have made it down from the trees and built things like cities and cineplexes. It should not, therefore, be as difficult as it is to explain to the average human male that while you, individual man, going about your daily business, eating crisps and playing BioShock 2, may not hate and hurt women, men as a group – men as a structure – certainly do. I do not believe that the majority of men are too stupid to understand this distinction, and if they are, we really need to step up our efforts to stop them running almost every global government.

Somehow, it is still hard to talk to men about sexism without meeting a wall of defensiveness that shades into outright hostility, even violence. Anger is an entirely appropriate response to learning that you're implicated in a system that oppresses women but the solution isn't to direct that anger back at women. The solution isn't to shut down debate by accusing us of 'reverse sexism', as if that will somehow balance out the problem and stop you feeling so uncomfortable.

Sexism should be uncomfortable. It is painful and enraging to be on the receiving end of misogynist attacks, and it is also painful to watch them happen and to know that you're implicated, even though you never chose to be. You're supposed to react when you're told that a group you are a member of is actively fucking over other human beings, in the same way that you're supposed to react when a doctor hammers your knee to test your nerves. If it doesn't hurt, something is horribly wrong.

Saying that 'all men are implicated in a culture of sexism' – all men, not just some men – may sound like an accusation.

In fact, it's a challenge. You, individual man, with your individual dreams and desires, did not ask to be born into a world where being a boy gave you social and sexual advantages over girls. You don't want to live in a world where women get raped and then told they provoked it in a court of law, where women's work is poorly paid or unpaid, where we are called sluts and whores for demanding simple sexual equality. You did not choose any of this. What you do get to choose, right now, is what happens next.

You can choose, as a man, to help create a fairer world for women, and for men, too. You can choose to challenge misogyny and sexual violence wherever you see them. You can choose to take risks and spend energy supporting women, promoting women, treating the women in your life as true equals. You can choose to stand up and say no, and every day more men and boys are making that choice. The question is – will you be one of them?

NAMING PATRIARCHY

For many centuries, money, power and the ability to create large amounts of random bloody carnage has been concentrated in the hands of a few white European men, usually the richest and most well connected. Between them, these men represent only a fraction of the total male population, and yet every man and boy is expected to aspire to be just like them, and every woman is expected to aspire to be in their company. There's a simple word for this system. The word is 'patriarchy'. 'Patriarchy' does not mean 'the rule of men'. It means 'the rule of fathers' – literally, the rule of powerful heads of household over everybody else in society. Men further down the social chain were expected to be content with having power over women in order to make up for their lack of control over the rest of their lives.

The word 'patriarchy' is a particularly hard one to hear, describing as it does a structure of economic and sexual oppression centuries old in which only a few men were granted power. Patriarchy: not the rule of men, but the rule of fathers and of father figures. Most individual men do not rule very much, and they never have. Most individual men don't have a lot of power, and now the small amount of social and sexual superiority they held over women is being questioned. That must sting. Benefiting from patriarchy doesn't make you a bad person, although it does very little to help you be a better one. The test of character, as with everyone who finds themselves in a position of power over others, is what you do with that realisation.

Patriarchy, throughout most of human history, is what has oppressed and constrained men and boys as well as women. Patriarchy is a top-down system of male dominance that is established with violence or with the threat of violence. When feminists say 'patriarchy hurts men too', this is what we really mean. Patriarchy is painful, and violent, and hard for men to opt out of, and bound up with the economic and class system of capitalism. I've found that when I speak to men about gender and violence, the word 'patriarchy' is one of the hardest for them to bear.

Modern economics creates few winners, so a lot of men are left feeling like losers – and a loser is the last thing a man ought to be. Women don't want to be with losers. Losers aren't real men, desirable men, strong men, and if neoliberalism is creating more losers, it must be because men aren't being properly appreciated, and it's probably the fault of feminism, not fiscal mismanagement. Neoliberalism may have set up vast swathes of people to fail, but the real problem cannot be a crisis of capitalism, so it must be a crisis of gender.

Across the global north and south, people are realising how they have been cheated of social, financial and personal power by their elected representatives and unelected elites – but young men still learn that their identity and virility depends on being powerful. What I hear most from the men and boys who contact me is that they feel less powerful than they had hoped to be, and they don't know who to blame.

MASCULINITY IS CRISIS

It's a hot August night and significant parts of London are on fire. For three hours, we've been holed up in the front room of my boyfriend's shared house watching Croydon burn, waiting for the sounds of breaking glass and howling sirens to come closer up the high street. It is the third night of the English riots, and all over the city, young men and a few young women have come out to loot shops and fight the police, organising online, swarming out of the inner-city areas that TV cameras only visit when there's been a shooting, which in this case, there has – a young father shot dead at point-blank range by police in Tottenham. These young people come from areas where police harassment is a daily reality and every small service that made life bearable – the education support, the youth centres and the jobseekers' allowance – is being cut in an austerity drive that has left the salaries of the super-rich untouched. But we are assured that there is nothing political about these riots. The problem is young men, particularly young black boys, and their lack of discipline. It's not poverty and it's not the police. It must be masculinity gone mad.

Already on the radio, politicians and talking heads are speaking of a 'crisis of masculinity'. Fear of testosterone poisoning is the final posture of a kind of class hatred that can't face itself in the mirror, since managing and directing the energy of young men has always been about maintaining social order. It's obvious to anyone desperate to ignore political reality that the young men tearing up the tarmac in Ealing and Tottenham and throwing makeshift Molotovs at police in Brixton and Hackney didn't have strong male role models, weren't beaten enough as children, weren't real men, calm, orderly men, like the skinny-jean-wearing, Kasabian-listening sons of every political commentator freaking out on the news. Every time night falls and the inner-city kids come out to smash up another high street, the panicked media narrative disintegrates again, social media flashes and judders like the inside of an acid trip and nobody knows what's going on.

I am a journalist. I need to cover this story, find out what's happening to the city that I love. But I'm trapped in the living room because my boyfriend won't let me leave the house.

I'm a journalist and I'm prepared to take silly risks to do my job, and right now he isn't letting me. He says he has to keep me safe, even against my will.

Violence happens when people are frightened that somebody's about to take away their power. I have understood something new about men tonight, but it's not what they're saying on the news.

In most search engines, 'masculinity in' autocompletes to 'crisis'. The terms are so often connected that one can rarely talk about modern masculinity without acknowledging the sorry state it's in, the once-powerful beast languishing on the slab waiting to be put out of its misery. We discuss the sorry state of men, real men, men's men, dominant, powerful men, in lowered voices, lest we incite the vicious bitchwrath of the straw feminists.

In the year 2000, as Susan Faludi reported in *Stiffed*, 'As the nation wobbled toward the millennium, its pulse takers seemed to agree that a domestic apocalypse was underway: American manhood was under siege. Men on trial, the headlines cried, the trouble with boys, are men necessary? Maybe manhood can recover.'[2] More than a decade later, the same headlines still circulate: boys in crisis, testosterone on the wane, girls overtaking boys, how will men cope?

Masculinity, of course, is not in crisis – to a large degree, masculinity *is* crisis. Whether or not an oppressive system of social control is malfunctioning depends entirely on whether you expect it to be concerned with making a large number of people happy and fulfilled, which the postures of masculinity have never been designed to do. If modern masculinity is keeping men, particularly young men, in a state of anxious desperation, lonely and isolated, unable to express their true feelings or live the lives they really want, taking out their social and sexual frustration on women rather than understanding it as a systemic effect of elitism inequality, then masculinity is functioning perfectly well. It is, in fact, in tip-top shape.

Women, it seems, are allowed to talk only about their gender. Men are allowed to talk about absolutely anything except their gender. Discussing what it means to be a man is tacitly forbidden in most social circles. Masculinity functions rather like the film *Fight Club*, in that the first rule of Man Club is you do not talk about Man Club.

Barbara Ehrenreich, in her excellent cultural study *The Hearts of Men*, dates the loss of this pact of the patriarchal family deal back to the Beat generation of writers and radicals, 'the short-lived apotheosis of the male rebellion'[3] in which 'two strands of male protest – one directed against the white-collar work world and the other against the suburbanised family life that work was supposed to support – come together in the first all-out critique of American consumer culture.'[4] The Beats, in common with Hugh Hefner and the burgeoning cultural ideal of the Playboy bachelor that would eventually lead to such cult creations as James Bond, relied on 'rejection of the pact that the family wage system rested on',[5] whereby men were obliged to seek paid employment to support women's unpaid work, and the labour of both would be sealed in a system of sexual bargaining. If you're thinking that this sounds like a shit gig, you're not alone – and when many modern commentators speak of the loss of the 'traditional male breadwinner' role, they are speaking of a social arrangement that came to horrify both men and women in the mid-century when they realised there might be other options. Men's flight from traditional commitment, however, was never met by a concomitant idea of liberating women from domesticity. The notion that women, too, might be ambivalent about homemaking never came up. Suddenly, tying men down to the traditional home became women's full-time job.

'Traditional masculinity', like 'traditional femininity', is about control. It is a way of managing behaviour. There are two big secrets about 'traditional masculine power' that mainstream culture does not want us to discuss, and it is imperative that we discuss them honestly – men and women, boys and girls and everyone else pinned in painfully by the social straitjacket of 'traditional masculinity'. The first big secret is this: most men have never really been powerful. Throughout human history, the vast majority of men have had almost no structural power, except over women and children. In fact, power over women and children – technical and physical dominance within the sphere of one's own home – has been the sop offered to men who had almost no power outside of it.

One of the saddest things about modern society is that it has made us understand masculinity as something toxic and violent, associated with domination, control and savagery, being hungry for power and money and acquisitive, abusive sex. Part of the project of feminism is to free men as well as women from repressive stereotypes. Only some young men, of course. Few tears are being shed or water cannons mustered for the crises in masculinity that may or may not be occurring on private yachts and in the dormitories of elite boarding schools.

The second big secret about the Golden Age of

Masculinity, of course, is that it never really existed. There have always been men who were too poor, too queer, too sensitive, too disabled, too compassionate or simply too clever to fit in with whatever flavour of violent heterosexuality their society relied upon to keep its wars fought, its factories staffed and its women in check. Something does seem to be changing now, however: the myth just doesn't work for enough people any more.

The truth is that one of the main reasons young women are doing a little better in this recession than young men is that they are more exploitable, and more willing to let employers take advantage, because that's what good girls do. Men are burdened with too much ego for the kind of jobs that are going. 'One of the benefits that oppression confers upon the oppressors is that the most humble among them is made to feel superior.'[6] Thus, a poor man working a job he hated could once expect to feel, at the very least, superior to his wife and children, to be master of his home even if he was treated like a slave outside it. That is no longer a privilege guaranteed to any man who keeps his head down, although it remains a perk of the job for a good many.

It is difficult for men not to grow up with the expectation of power over women – even when that power is supposed to be benign, loving power, strong power, the power to protect and dominate. Almost every story boys get to read casts them as the hero and women and girls as supporting characters, mothers and wives and girlfriends. Culture has not yet adjusted to stop promising men the beautiful sidekick, the lovely princess, the silent, smiling companion as a reward for whatever trials life throws their way. Women, by contrast, although we still cast ourselves in that supporting role all too often, are no longer mandated into it by law and lack of medical technology.

The power of individual men over individual women is more embattled today than it has ever been – and as a consequence, it is more vengeful and more fetishised, especially in pornography, where hurting and humiliating women has become how sex is done. What men want is assumed to be basic, brute and uncomplicated. Beer and blow jobs and raw meat, preferably pulled off the steer as it runs past and deep-fried in testosterone.

It is extremely tricky to pinpoint what men actually want, for three major reasons: firstly, there are three and a half billion men and boys on this planet, and the Internet has proved conclusively that a great many of them are excited and troubled by a lot of very strange things indeed.

Secondly, while men are permitted to express desire in a way many women and girls are not, that desire is very specifically directed and any deviance punished, often with violence. The passion of young men is policed twice over, by fear of masculinity gone feral on the one hand and by homophobia on the other. In many parts of the global north we have arrived, however tentatively, at a position where outright violence against gay men and lesbians is considered backward, and where gay people have fought successfully for the same rights to marry, cohabit and die in war zones as their straight counterparts. This is to be celebrated, but homophobia is about far more than merely punishing people who fuck their own sex. For young men in particular, violent homophobia is used to manage every aspect of gendered behaviour.

Thirdly, the difference between what a man is supposed to want, what he thinks he ought to want and what he really wants is muddled, just as it is for women. It may take a man years to admit to himself that he just doesn't like beer. Or maybe he finds himself attracted to chubby or less stereotypically attractive women, or to loud, difficult, masculine women, or other men, but won't let himself pursue them because of what his friends might say. Desire is socially constructed: what the heart and groin and stomach want is brokered by the basic desire to fit in and not make a fuss.

What right have women to speak about men and what they feel and desire? We have every right, particularly as men have been speaking about women, writing about women, making laws about women and trying to figure out what we want and feel for so many years, with women rarely permitted to speak back. We have every right, and until men start speaking about their own experience of gender and sex honestly, we may even have a duty. Because gender and desire are the sole topics on which women are permitted any sort of public expertise. From a young age, I was asked to speak on countless panels as a representative of what 'women' thought, as if I was plugged into some sort of magical hive vagina that meant I knew what all women were thinking at any given time.

So here are a few of the things that most men aren't allowed to want: to be taken care of. To be cuddled. To do creative work that will not make money. To go out to a club dressed in tight pants and thigh-high boots. To cry in public.

To be a full-time parent. To cry in private. To be fucked. To play with make-up. To have their vulnerabilities acknowledged. To care what other people think. To care as a career. To paint their nails and bedrooms day-glo orange. To listen unironically to Taylor Swift. To dance with abandon. To have women as friends. To meet women as equals. To know that being a man is as uncompulsory a constitutive quality of their selfhood as being a woman is to anyone born that way.

Here's another thing most men aren't allowed to want: deep and lasting social change.

IT DOESN'T GET BETTER

May 2012. Three in the morning on a red-eye bus through Pennsylvania, at some godawful service stop in the middle of nowhere. The bus is full of young men in their teens and early twenties snuggled together under coats, or wrapped in blankets in the aisle. All of them are activists from the Occupy movement, heading to Chicago for the NATO protests. Many of them are, additionally, homeless, jobless and multiply damaged, and have taken the opportunity of a free bus ride because they have nowhere else to sleep. These are the young people to whom liberals everywhere are looking, however briefly, to sketch out a new politics in chalk on the pavement, and they are precisely the young people for whom the simple story of escape, the myth that if you only work hard and get to college and stick out the tough stuff you will be rescued from your social circumstances, didn't work, will never work again. They are not all right.

Forty-five lost boys on a journey between uncertainties, off to stake a claim in the world, however small.

If being a man means being powerful and power means the ability to have an impact on society, situations of rapid social change have always been in part about boys getting a chance to show off – and that's not necessarily a bad thing. In the student movements and occupations that helped form my politics, I saw boys hungry and anxious to find themselves, to prove themselves men.

In those same spaces, I saw those same boys having to deal with the uneasy fact that in these precious transformation zones, it wasn't just people who looked like them realising their own power as citizens. Women, people of colour and queer people were there too, and they shared that hunger for social justice.

The important thing about that sort of trauma is not just that it is survivable. We did survive, after all, most of us, though I can't honestly say that it always got better. The important thing about that sort of trauma is that it is the material out of which change is made.

The young America that created the Occupy movement is the same young America that has for years been in the grip of an epidemic of suicide and self-injury. Rates of suicide among fifteen-to-twenty-four-year-olds in the USA have tripled over the past thirty years. After a brief respite, those rates have been rising since the recession hit in 2008, as youth unemployment has soared to 2.7 million. When Émile Durkheim wrote *Suicide* in 1897, he observed that the older a person was, the more likely he or she was to take his or her own life.[7] Durkheim believed that there was a straightforward reason for this: the young usually have more life ahead of them to lose, and more reason to hope for a drastic change in their circumstances.[8] In the past sixty years, however, the correlation between age and suicide has become more complex.

What does it take to make a young person despair?

On 9 September 2010, Billy Lucas went out to his grandmother's barn in Greenberg, Indiana, and hung himself. He was fifteen years old, and one of the few non-white kids in the small-town high school where he had suffered homophobic bullying for over a year before he took his own life. There was nothing out of the ordinary about Billy's tragedy: last year in America thousands of teenagers killed themselves, and just like last year and the year before that, young gay, bisexual and transsexual people were particularly at risk, with suicide rates over quadruple those of heterosexual youth. That autumn, at least ten young Americans who were gay or lesbian or who, like Billy, had been bullied mercilessly for not conforming to expected stereotypes of sexuality and gender performance, took their own lives. What was unusual was what happened next.

The popular advice columnist Dan Savage made a video with his husband, telling gay teenagers to hang in there, promising them, in words that would become a worldwide anti-suicide slogan, that 'It Gets Better'.[9] 'I wish I could have talked to that kid for five minutes and been able to tell him that,' Savage told NPR, after the clip went viral around the world, prompting thousands of others to tell their own stories of hope. 'But I would never get permission to talk to these kids or an invitation to talk to high school or middle schools.

And it occurred to me that I was waiting for permission that I didn't need any more . . . We could talk about having survived bullying and our lives now and offer these kids hope.'[10]

Celebrities and politicians from across the English-speaking world jumped on the 'It Gets Better' bandwagon: what began as a well-positioned campaign quickly became a way to prove your credentials as a progressive public figure. President Obama's contribution was one of the finest made, and it worked precisely because the Obama brand has long been about 'offering hope' without going into too much detail about what the road from here to hope might look like.

From the start, the kind of hope on offer with 'It Gets Better' was specific and familiar: leave Indiana. Leave. Leave Alabama. Leave Antrim and Teesside. Leave all of those small close-minded towns behind and go to college, move to the big city and join the creative upper-middle classes any way you can, if you can. 'It Gets Better' is neoliberal mythmaking writ large, not just a plea for emotional resilience but a manifesto for economic compliance, the promise that if you only work hard and tough it all out, you'll have a better life than your parents had. It's a promise that a majority of Americans no longer believe will be true for the next generation. It's a promise that erases class, race and gender difference, and as austerity clamps down those differences are becoming impossible to ignore.

Savage's message may have been a desperate fairy tale, but fairy tales have their uses, especially when you're scrambling to think of something to say to stop an anonymous child somewhere in the world damaging themselves beyond help. When you're talking to a person having suicidal thoughts, you will say anything – literally anything – that sounds like a plausible reason not to give up on life, you will promise them unicorns and magical lands at the end of the rainbow and secure jobs after college and other such happy fantasies. Crisis talk, however, is no long-term solution to inequality, and crisis talk is all the Obama generation has had to cling to for five years and more.

As rousing slogans go, 'It Gets Better' is hardly fist-pumping. The painful fact remains that for LGBT youth it gets a whole lot better a whole lot faster if you're white, middle-class and moneyed, like every other empty neoliberal promise ever tossed at millions of lonely, hurting kids. For many young people – for young people like Billy Lucas – life is actually a whole lot more complicated.

Sometimes 'It Gets Better' isn't enough. Sometimes you need to make it better right now.

At the end of the Occupy movement in New York, I stood on a side street in the early evening in Lower Manhattan, watching the bus-kids unroll their sleeping bags and cardboard pallets. They were the last vestiges of the Zucotti Park camp, the lost kids from all over America who came to New York the prevous winter and had nowhere else to go. They hadn't gone home, because they couldn't. On the pavement across from Wall Street, they slept outdoors while the weather held, chalking slogans about corporate greed on the concrete, refusing to leave, and when they got too noisy, too rowdy, the police swept in and dragged them away in ones and twos. A lot of them were runaways. Many of them were queer or transsexual: nineteen-year-old Rina, Envy and Franklin, young lovers who met in the Washington camp nine months ago; Little Sean from Philadelphia, curled in a crusty sleeping bag, his cornrows poking out, who burnt a dollar he really needed just to show me how much he hated money, and then told me how his parents kicked him out. Across the street, armed police took shifts to watch them sleep, occasionally charging in with cuffs and pointed guns to arrest them if they got too rowdy. These kids waited for it to get better. It didn't.

Sometimes young people get sick of waiting for things to get better, and that's when they start to fight back. Over two years of following the new student protests and Occupy protests in Britain, Europe and the United States, what struck me most profoundly is how these movements are driven by those same lost, vulnerable young people for whom the promise of a better future rotted with the recession. In the temporary refugee camps that sprung up in New York and London and Washington and Chicago, I met countless homeless runaways in their teens and early twenties. Interviewing them for article after article on the economic focus of the protests, I began to see patterns many mainstream journalists seemed to me to be ignoring on purpose, because they didn't fit any neat story about dirty hippies or passionate anti-capitalist revolutionaries. The scars on arms and shoulders, the marks of knives and cigarettes on tender skin, some of them self-inflicted, some, I was told, anything but. The dirt under their fingernails. The excitement in their eyes at finding something to belong to, at finding love and acceptance after years of frustration and rejection.

So much of the Occupy movement, with its parades, its crazy costumes and its proud declarations of solidarity, was like a great big coming-out party. Across the world, storytelling was an enormous part of the uprisings of 2011. Against the single story of an individual striving towards, inevitably, prosperity that has dominated the past thirty years of political inheritance in the West, people offered their own stories, hard, raw stories of debt and disease and disappointment.

Talking about trauma is a queer activity in every sense, particularly for men, when it is forbidden unless you're in a war movie. It allows us to reimagine the present. In the middle of a noisy demonstration on 17 November 2011, two days after the eviction of the first Occupy Camp at Zucotti Park, I saw something very special happen at the corner of Nassau and Pine in the Financial District. About two hundred people had gathered at the junction, pushed backwards by the police, and suddenly they began to step forward one by one and give impromptu speeches about how the American Dream had failed them. One was a schoolteacher who barely made her rent; another was a disabled parent struggling with no health insurance; a blue-collar worker whose home had been foreclosed; a young student facing lifelong education debts.

I arrived just after it began, and I have no idea if it was pre-planned, but everywhere people were nudging each other forwards, stepping into the circle that had formed to share their own small, hurting piece of the global economic crisis. To say that the stories were tragic would imply that they were somehow extraordinary, but this was ordinary suffering and everyday rage, the sort of feelings that Americans in particular are meant to feel ashamed about owning in public. As these people shared their stories – quickly, because the NYPD were approaching with plasticuffs and billy-clubs – there was a sense of elation, a relief in finally being able to be open about the truth of their lives. Social change happens when the old stories we tell ourselves to survive are no longer sufficient, and we create new ones.

The anger of men-children shut out of the future they were promised can be productive. Those lost kids peopled Occupy Wall Street, fronted the student uprisings of the century's tweenage years with precocious sloganeering and red-hot rage.

I watched transfixed as the mournful young men I'd spent so long trying to drag out of the house and down to the dole office to fill in applications for jobs that weren't there were transfigured into adults. They stood taller. I watched them stand on steps of occupied squares and make speeches, and then I saw them stand aside so that women and people of colour could speak too, and that sacrifice of space and privilege was suddenly in the squares. In those few days between the opening up of the protest camps and the influx of police beating and arresting and loading tents and books into dumpster trucks to be pulped, there was space for everyone.

At least, that's how it seemed. But then the music stopped. The police came in with guns and gas to clear the camps, but even before they had done so, rancour and suspicion had settled in. You see, even in these temporary autonomous zones, in these brief magical spaces opening up across the world to let in freeloaders and free-thinkers and revolutionaries and lost kids to hold the space for as long as they could stand, even there, there was rape.

For three years after the groundswell of grassroots rage that swept the globe in 2011, the fledgling counterculture fractured and fractured again over its own inability to deal with male privilege and sexual violence. Groups split. Angry lines were drawn in ground that had only recently been reclaimed by the young and hungry. It was heartbreaking to watch.

In 2010, the world's most powerful activist, Julian Assange, was arrested on rape charges he refused even to answer, and marginalised men-children across the world held his face on posters, telling the carrion-feeding cameras come to feast on the still twitching carcass of the renascent left that state surveillance was immoral, that whistle-blowers should be protected – and that women lie.

At Occupy, women were raped in their tents and sexually assaulted at sit-ins. In Baltimore, in Dallas, in Cleveland, in Glasgow.[11] At Occupy London a prominent activist who was tried and acquitted for the rape of two female comrades kept a list of sexual conquests on the wall of his tent. The list began, according to his defence, 'as a joke with other men' at the camp.[12]

At the same time, the online dissident group Anonymous published a Survival Guide for Citizens in a Revolution,[13] intended, quite seriously, 'for citizens who feel they are about to be caught up in a violent uprising'. A whole page of the guide was dedicated to a ten-point plan for avoiding rape, including the following advice: 'try to appear undesirable and unattractive', 'never go out alone' and 'do not wear skirts'. The people who wrote this guide meant well, as do most men who instruct women to live in fear for their own good. The authors of the guide take pains to reassure us that these hypothetical circumstances are not normal: 'what might be okay in a stable society' – wearing clothes that show your thighs, for instance – 'will get you in deep trouble in times when there is no backed law enforcement'.

What is a stable society? I've never heard of one, never lived in one, not here, not anywhere. If women's bodies are fair game outside 'stable society' then hell, we're always fair game. Show me a society that's stable that isn't a miserable police state; show me law enforcement that gives less than two shits about protecting women from rape and assault if they're not wealthy and white.

Socialism without feminism is no socialism worth having, and men and boys are beginning to learn, slowly and painfully, that they cannot liberate themselves alone. Too many social movements have treated women, queer people and people of colour as collateral damage, telling us to swallow our suffering until the revolution is over – but somehow, that time never comes. This time is different. We are refusing to wait any longer, and we are taking the boys along, too.

CLOCKING IN, CHECKING OUT

The precious core of modern male privilege is time. It's the time to decide where your life is going before certain people start telling you it's effectively over. It's the time to make money, build a career, travel the world or just learn to play the trumpet really damn well before you even have to think about finding a partner and starting a family. It's the time to be young, to fuck up, to fail and start again. It's the time to get distinguished, rather than grow old. It's time.

By the time we hit our late twenties, women and girls are expected to have their shit more or less together. We are expected to have chosen the people around whom our life's work will revolve, to have made a plan and begun to put it into practice. The word 'young' stops being a prefix to 'woman' when we are spoken about in the third person. The women we see in the public eye, the women who are celebrated and held up as role models, are overwhelmingly very young, sometimes barely out of school. This is not the case for people living as men. Miley Cyrus is castigated for being a poor role model, but Justin Bieber can trash all the hotel rooms he likes. He's young. He'll learn.

I'm twenty-seven years old right now, and I'm barely a functional adult. I like ramen noodles and gin and staying up late having dramatic conversations on the Internet, and sometimes I just flip over yesterday's underwear because the washing isn't done. I have a tax-paying job and a blazer to wear to meetings and I'm grown up about contraception and healthcare, but that is no indication of any sustained ability to take responsibility for myself or any other human being. And yet family members are already starting to make worried noises about the time it's taking me to settle down and warm my ovaries up, even though I'm clearly in no position to take care of a baby, a boyfriend, or both. I still leave bright-pink hair dye all over the bathroom as if some cartoon character has been horribly slaughtered, but apparently, it's time to think baby.

Other women I know who write, make art or work in politics have begun to talk, in hushed and anxious tones, about the next ten years as a time of hard, adult choices in a way that I never hear from my male friends. None of us have the kind of high-flying jobs that would allow us to think in terms of 'having it all' – the man, the mortgage, the baby and the briefcase – and yet we still hear the ticking of the clock getting louder. The biological clock is a social idea. It is used to reinstitute a measure of compliance in women and girls. It tells us that any freedom we have is time-limited, that we can dance all night if we want, but midnight is approaching, and when the coach turns back into a pumpkin, we'd better make sure it's dropped us somewhere safe.

Whether or not we ever plan to have children, women's professional potential and social value is still subtly measured along the timescale of our fertility. We are expected to slide quietly off the escalator of money and power in our early to mid-thirties, and if we refuse to do so, we are considered superwomen or cold, grasping bitches, or both. The same cultural logic that tells us that women are most desirable and exciting in our teens and early twenties, when we barely know how to order a drink, tells men and boys not to hurry – they have things to sell that aren't based on their youth and physical charms. When they get bigger and uglier and happier, they will only be more powerful. Women fear that we will become invisible. We know that, like Cinderella, our time is running out. Men are told that there is time enough.

Those ten extra years make all the difference. They are the ten years in which we get to fuck up, be young, damage ourselves and heal again and, if we're lucky, try to build something out of the debris of lust and dreams we accrete like limpets clinging to the underside of time. Men don't get told that the best years are over just as they're starting to get the hang of being here.

When I think of the lost young men I have known and loved, the ones who made it and the ones who didn't, a fist of rage and sadness clenches and unclenches under my ribcage. When I think of all the brilliant, passionate, scared young men, mostly poor, many queer and of colour, who didn't get the chance to make something out of the great gift of those years, I want to shake them in frustration. The tragedy of male privilege is that it is no longer a guarantee of health and happiness, if it ever was.

A HISTORY OF VIOLENCE

How should we forgive men who have hurt us? Is it even possible? It is 2009. I'm in a chain coffee-shop, space that is not just neutral but nowhere, a rash of familiar decor infesting the walls, waiting for a man. Waiting for a particular man. People who ask why I like coffee shops so much usually haven't had their arse grabbed in a bar. I'm particularly keen for that not to happen today, because I am maintaining a tricky equilibrium between loving compassion and the impulse to smack the next unsuspecting, undeserving male human I see in the face and shout incoherently until he develops some goddamn humanity. I buy a cup of truly appalling chain-coffee-shop tea, plant my feet on the floor in the corner, and wait.

The man I'm waiting for is late. When he arrives he apologises, although not too much. We talk about how he's doing, how my boyfriend is doing, how his wife is enjoying her new job. Years ago, this man raped me after a party while I was passed out on his bed. I'm here to see what he has to say for himself, because I am pretty sure that he has chosen to believe that what he did wasn't rape, because he's a good guy, and good guys don't do that shit to teenage girls. They don't fuck them unconscious without a condom and infect them with something mercifully treatable. Did I go to the police? Did I hell. I thought I was a stupid slag who deserved it. I was afraid I wouldn't be believed, by the law or by mutual friends, and that assessment proved entirely correct.

It is too late now to make amends to the damaged kid that I used to be. That girl is gone, and someone else is here instead, someone older and uglier and angrier. The friends I lost after I dared to speak of it the first time because he was a charming, respected older man and I was a drunk teen slut are not friends I wish to regain. Nor am I particularly concerned for his immortal soul. I just want to stop it happening again to somebody else, and now word has reached me of a similar incident, so here I am, stirring my tea like a cauldron and wishing I could do magic.

I make some tight-lipped pleasantries and arrive, via a circuitous route that ambles around gosh-that-was-an-interesting-night, at the point. It is remarkably difficult to tell somebody, in person and without prevaricating, that they have raped you. It is difficult to explain in an even tone to someone who likes to think of himself as a decent human being that he has probably hurt you, but you must keep your voice soft and steady, because something between fear and fury is boiling in the back of your throat and you're worried about what might happen if you let it loose. For minutes that feel like months, he just doesn't get it.

And then he gets it.

I have never watched a human face flush and alter quite so curiously as this man's does when I explain why what he did was rape, and that it was unacceptable. He stammers that he is sorry. I thank him, and ask him not to do it again, and then I get to my feet, and push past the table, and walk away. For now, this man is sorry and ashamed, and there aren't enough jails in the world to hold the hundreds of thousands just like him, perfectly ordinary chaps, a lot less clever than they think they are, who cannot contemplate that they, enlightened modern souls, could really do such harm. Rape, abuse and violence are something that evil men do, and they are not evil men.

Later that night, I receive an enraged email from his wife. I have done something terrible, something truly unforgivable: I have upset her husband.

And that's when I get it. The worst thing we can possibly do in situations like this is make men feel uncomfortable. Acknowledging the enormity of male violence, the staggering scale of entitlement, would require a change in perspective so massive that it's easier just to shut up and not talk about it, and isolate anyone who does. We don't want to hear it.

It can be terribly uncomfortable for men to hear about misogyny, particularly their own. Unfortunately for them, as soon as they start to think and speak about gender they often run into one awful, unshakeable fact: how much men as a whole have hurt women. That means that it's hugely difficult for men to talk about masculinity without coming to terms with how frightening and aggressive masculinity in its modern form has come to be. It's frightening. It's going to hurt.

Here's what hurts, too: 8 per cent of men admit committing acts that meet the legal definition of rape or attempted rape.[14] More than one in five men report 'becoming so sexually aroused that they could not stop themselves from having sex, even though the woman did not consent'.[15] Rape and sexual violence are routine. Ritualised misogyny is so normalised that we need a radical redefinition of how men and women relate, and the traumatic beginnings of that redefinition are causing casualties on both sides. When rape is raised in the press, the concern is always for the man's reputation – which is considered of more value than a woman's autonomy. Women ruin lives with their lies, we are repeatedly told – men's lives, the only lives that matter. In fact, what is being ruined by women's refusal to remain mute is the illusion of sexual equality. Those who are so invested in the status quo that they would keep women silent when we try to speak about power, privilege and violence should ask themselves what it really means to be a man.

There's a playground legend that says that men think about sex every six seconds. For all that, they rarely get to speak about sexuality and what it means with anything approaching honesty. Men are supposed to fuck violently and on cue, to lust without reason, to barter crumbs of affection in exchange for access to sex with women, which they'll take by force when denied. There is no language for softness, for searching, for play. Men as well as women are taught that male sexuality is toxic and dangerous – and at the same time utterly natural. Men learn that there is a deep well of violence inside them that is connected to sexuality, and it cannot be controlled, only contained.

A lot of men find this monolithic portrayal of their own sexuality extremely disturbing. Men who are gay or bisexual, of course, are used to not seeing their own sexuality represented or catered to in the mainstream other than obliquely, jokily, as a counterfoil to the violently identikit heterosexuality that dominates our visual culture. But men who are attracted mainly to the opposite sex are also offered only one way to express themselves sexually, and that is in the manner of a barely tamed beast. I regularly receive emails from men and boys who are completely unsure how to relate to that stereotype, but afraid of rejection, by their peers or their partners, if they don't.

Here's what I'd like to say to those men. It's okay to be afraid. It's okay not to know what you're supposed to be, or how you're supposed to behave. You're not allowed to question what it means to be a man, or even raise the possibility that there might be a question to ask, because if you did, if anyone did, then we might get answers. We might discover that what we all liked to think of as 'masculinity' is in fact a front, that 'masculinity' is actually fragile, and vulnerable, and hurting, and nothing more than human.

Real men aren't meant to ask questions. Real men hit things with hammers or blast them with lasers until the problem goes away. But what if the problem is your own heart? What if the problem is just a sense, deep inside you, that something is desperately wrong? Hammers and lasers are still an option, of course, but so is taking your own distress seriously, sitting with it, not trying to submerge it with chemicals or recreational misogyny.

It is, of course, not the job of women, or of feminist activists, to fix men's problems for them. Even if it were, there are a great many women out there who are deeply traumatised by their interactions with men and want nothing more to do with them, and that is very much their right. I have compassion for the small school of feminism that believes that the only way to deal with male violence is to shout at men and boys until they stop, and I have, in the past, found myself part of that school of thought. No longer.

Thinking in a new way about sex, gender and power can help men to process their gendered pain. Unfortunately for them, as soon as they start to think and speak about gender they often run into one awful, unshakeable fact: how much men as a whole have hurt women. Realising the full extent of male violence against women comes as a painful shock to any man of conscience. That means that it's hugely difficult for men to talk about masculinity without coming to terms with how frightening and aggressive masculinity in its modern form has come to be.

Being on the receiving end of prejudice is always hurtful, whether or not that prejudice is practical. Women understand that men are trained to see them as a category, as a social problem to be dealt with, rather than as individual humans. When men realise that women often see them in exactly the same way – to whit, as hostile territory – they often react with pain and anger.

Social heterosexuality has been allowed to remain a process of mutual dehumanisation. Hence the ongoing debate over whether men and women can 'really' be friends with each other 'without sex getting in the way'. The truly telling part of this perennial non-controversy is not just that it is entertained as a serious prospect, but that sexuality is assumed to destroy any possibility of friendship. Thus, any person who you might want to see naked is on fundamentally hostile territory, to be conquered rather than understood.

What almost all men and boys want – in fact, what almost all human beings want – is to feel useful and needed and loved. One of the quiet tragedies of our age is that we're still telling young men that the only way they can be useful is either by earning a pile of money and bringing it home to a grateful, pliant wife who rewards you with dull, dutiful sex and home-baked brownies in return for a lifetime of financial security, or by fighting – and possibly dying – in a war very far from home.

In the real world, most men have never had lives like that, and today more and more of the wars are being fought by robots that can set wedding parties on fire without flinching and, should they fail to return, will leave no widows behind. But men still want to feel useful, needed and loved.

At least, that's what they tell me in their letters. I would despair, if I didn't get so many letters. For every man who takes time out of his busy schedule of hating himself to tell me I'm an evil, frigid Feminazi who deserves to choke on his vengeful erection, there is another who just wants to know what he can do to help prevent rape. Or who is upset because no matter how hard he tries, he can't get a job in this recession and he feels like less of a man because of it. Sometimes I get emails from male college students shyly confiding that they think they might be feminists and is that all right, in the way that one might ask whether or not the purple rash they've developed is quite normal. Not one of these men has expressed a desire to be a 'provider', but there is an anguish in their need to communicate.

A great many men and boys do not want to be 'providers', or 'hard men', just like a great many men and boys do not want to dominate women as they have been taught to do. Almost all of the young men and boys I've been close to in my life have wanted something quite different. Much as I'd like to put that down to my unending, knicker-moistening attraction to limp-wristed, nerdy bisexual communists with funny hair and sad eyes, I've known and loved enough of them to understand that it's a little more complicated than that. There are more and more men and boys who are failing to see any part of themselves reflected in the mirrored cage of what Jackson Katz calls 'The Man Box'.[16] They want to crack open the cage, and join the others.

Because there have always been the others. That's the last great secret of this supposed 'golden age of masculinity' that's been destroyed by feminism: it never really existed in the first place, because at every stage of human history, no matter what contorted, narrow vision of 'manhood' society relied upon to keep its wars fought, its fields tilled, its factories staffed and its women in check, there have been men who would not or could not conform. Men who were too poor, or too queer, or too compassionate. Men who were too physically small, too shy, too disabled, too sensitive or too gentle to bear the clunking fist that was supposed to squash them all into a single understanding of what it meant to be 'manly'. Men who were big and brawny and wanted nothing more than to run away to the city and paint pictures. Men who loved sex but didn't want to get married or have kids. Men who wanted to be submissive to women, or to other men, and didn't consider it a weakness. Men whose skill was in caring for children and the elderly. Men who just weren't terribly impressed with the prospect of spending forty years hitting things with sticks for a living. Those men have always existed, quietly giving the lie to the notion that there has ever been one way of 'being a man'.

The reason for a compassionate feminist approach to men is not to spare their feelings. Quite the opposite. Compassion is necessary precisely because to live full lives as we move towards a society that treats women as fully human, men will be required to see themselves and their experience in a new and painful light.

The sort of compassion that is useful to men and boys seeking to escape a world of violence, misogyny and emotional constipation is not the compassion of a priest who forgives sins, but of a doctor who looks at a suffering idiot who waited too long to get an oozing wound checked out and says, firmly and accurately: I'm afraid this is going to hurt.

Of course it's going to hurt. But then, it hurts already. The deep pain that the twisted mess of modern masculinity causes a great number of men is not often spoken about, because if it were permitted expression it would not be felt as rage or hate, but as fear and loathing, as confusion and self-doubt, or simply not being sure what the fuck we're supposed to be these days. And that's just not manly.

What we are asking men to do is hard. Let's be perfectly clear: we have created a society in which it is structurally difficult and existentially stressful for any male person not to behave like a complete and utter arsehole. The fact that not a few of them manage to be decent humans anyway is to their credit.

The gains that women have made in the workplace, our new relative freedom from the obligation to get married, bear children and submit to male power at home and work are framed uncomplicatedly as a loss to men and boys. It's as if there were a fixed amount of equality in the world and giving more to women automatically meant taking it away from men. Freedom doesn't work like that. Freedom is one of the few things in the world that enriches the people who give it to you, even if they give it unwillingly. Men of conscience have no idea how much they will love living in a world where women are permitted to live, work and fuck as free and equal agents, in a world where humanity comes before gender.

Feminism must address men's issues not as an afterthought, but directly, and passionately, because right now there is a conspiracy of silence around men and gender. If male identity is to stand a chance, men and boys must accept that the old distributive model of patriarchal power is gone. It never really existed for most people anyway. What the men of tomorrow must do is let it go with grace. Retain some dignity over a perceived loss of power, and people who are not men might speak to you honestly about what real powerlessness looks like.

Please understand that I have no intention of making feminism one jot less threatening, or persuading men that feminism will not change their lives because it already has, and it will continue to do so before we're done, and that's a good thing. It's not that you can't afford feminism. However broke you are, you can't afford a world without it. And I can't wait for us to get started.

Seriously. I can't wait. I can't wait for us to meet one another as equals. I can't wait for the liberation of human potential that's got to come when one half of the human race does not live in fear of the other. Where we can wear what we want and love who we like with no anticipation of violence. Those who are creating it, men and women and everyone else, do so by trying to live more freely than is strictly safe in this monstrosity we call modern life.

With every passing year I meet more men and boys who are as sick of restrictive gender norms as the rest of us, and who are prepared to do something about it, to live lives which make space for difference, and to stand up for those who do the same. The task is not easy. To reject the violent rituals that come with being raised male is to risk violence, to risk making mistakes and looking stupid, to risk having one's pride hurt profoundly, and I am moved by the courage of the men and boys in my life who take those risks. They are the strong ones. They are the ones who know that true strength involves the capacity to adapt, because when you fall, if you can't bend, you break. They are the ones with the power to make the world new. And as long as I remain a political creature, I will stand in solidarity with those men.

3

Anticlimax

A revolutionary in every bedroom cannot fail
to shake up the status quo.
Shulamith Firestone, *The Dialectic of Sex*

SLUT TALK

Here are the situations in which I have been called a slut: when I have spoken out or spoken up. When I have had the audacity to ask for money or fame instead of keeping my legs and mouth shut like a nice girl should. When I have been political in public. When I have left my bed unmade and floors unscrubbed and gone out making trouble. When I have taken too many lovers and prioritised my work over making them feel special. And finally, most incongruously, while fucking.

I am consistently stunned by the proportion of otherwise polite men and boys who get off on calling women bitches and whores and sluts in bed. Nominally feminist and sex-positive men ask if they can say it; the less enlightened just spit it out. Slut. Whore. It seems to be a statement straight from the mind-set that any woman who really, truly consents to sex, who really wants to meet you in bed as an equal, must be a slag, a whore, taking it – always taking it – like a slut.

Porn has a lot to answer for when it comes to the semantic variety of sex talk. A language of violence slipping off the erotic vulgar tongue, where penetration is a woman's punishment for lust. If you like it, best pretend that you don't.[1] Let them castigate you for letting them fuck you while they do it.

Slut. It's a slur, but it shouldn't be.

Slut: just saying the word parts the lips a little too wide. The sloppy vowel-sound sloshed around the underside of the palate and then snatched back, too late, like some cast-off notion of reputation. Slut. It's fun to say and it's fun to be, as long as you abide by the principle that if you're going to break a rule, you may as well snap it over your knee, set fire to the pieces and run away. Slut. It's a word of power. I'm taking it back.

In the past, the word 'slut' was used simply to mean any woman who didn't behave: a woman who was 'dirty, untidy or slovenly', a slack servant girl, a woman who failed to keep her house in order and her legs closed before marriage, a woman who invited violence and contempt. Today, in a visual culture sodden with images of shorn and willing female bodies, a slut is any woman with the audacity to express herself sexually. That should tell you everything you need to know about modern erotic hypocrisy.

The Slutwalk phenomenon began in Toronto in 2011, after a local policeman instructed a group of female university students to stop 'dressing like sluts' if they didn't want to be raped,[2] a point of view not unique among men in positions of power. The global protests that followed have infected the imagination of women in cities around the world, from Dallas to Delhi, who are sick of being bullied and intimidated into sexual conformity.

We like to think that we live in a liberal, permissive society – that, if anything, the problem is that there is too much sex about. This is a cruel delusion. We live in a culture that is deeply confused about its erotic impulses; it bombards us with images of airbrushed models and celebrities writhing in a sterile haze of anhedonia while abstinence is preached at the heart of government.

If I could take a red pen and annotate the world, I would scrawl 'slut power' in letters too big to ignore.

For over a century, 'slut' has been a word of censure. It has been used to hurt people and make them ashamed. The word 'slut' has been used to control women and girls, queer people and poor people by making them feel ashamed of what they are and what they want. It keeps them in their place by telling them that wanting more than what they're allowed is shameful, whether that's a kiss from a stranger, a new world order or an extra slice of cake. 'Slut' tells us that our bodies are there to be kept in line. 'Slut' tells us that being hungry and horny and human is a bad thing, that we should control ourselves before someone does it for us. Slut is a word and an idea that desperately needs to be taken back.

Slut power means speaking up. It means standing your ground when those around you are attacked for wanting too much, demanding fair treatment, for taking up too much space. Women who are political are stereotyped as ugly, slutty and masculine because that's still the worst thing you can say to a woman who frightens you.

Being a slut doesn't have to mean fucking around, or fucking at all. It just means refusing to see desire as dirty. It means abandoning the pursuit of patriarchal approval as far as you can. Taking away its power to cut you down and shut you up.

Good little girls don't get off. I had the opportunity to learn this at an early age when I was thrown out of ballet class for teaching the other girls how to masturbate. I worked out how to touch myself by accident, and it was so much fun that I saw no reason not to share my thrilling discovery with my classmates.

When the teacher caught us, it was gently suggested to my mortified mother that maybe I wasn't suited to ballet. Perhaps one of the more masculine middle-class after-school activities, like judo or boxing, would be a better fit. I was terrible at martial arts. I'm weedy and easily startled and I hate hitting people. I just wanted to dance and have fun.

I have always been more interested in fucking than being fuckable. I'm drawn to others who feel the same. I can muddle through the rituals of sex appeal well enough when pressed, and retain a bewildered admiration for those women to whom it seems to come effortlessly, but for me sex is something you do, rather than something you stand around waiting for other people to do to you. I was too nerdy and shy to get a shag at school, but as soon as I left home, I tossed my virginity aside like ballast and soared off hunting for pleasure and adventure.

It stuns me that female desire is still taboo. The notion that women and girls might want sex for its own sake, rather than suffer it in exchange for money or status or security, is still an idea that is resisted by society at large.

We are not supposed to crave sweetness and danger and the scent of sweat on skin.

In Britain, the release of an official report declaring that girls are being too 'sexualised'[3] has coincided with parliamentary lobbies for young women to be 'taught to say no'.[4] Join the dots with police officers telling women that 'no' is insufficient if they happen not to be dressed like a nun and an ugly picture begins to form. What we're looking at is a concerted cultural backlash against female sexual liberation.

Sex is not the problem. Sexism is the problem. Arbitrary moral divisions are being renewed between 'innocent' women and 'sluts'. Young women, in particular, are expected to look hot and available at all times, but if we dare to express desires of our own, we are mocked, shamed and threatened with sexual violence, which, apparently, has nothing to do with the men who inflict it and everything to do with the length of skirt we have on. Some of us have had enough.

Faced with savage public opprobrium, told that our sexuality is dirty and dangerous, some young women are keen to reclaim 'slut', to celebrate its implications of bad behaviour, to refuse to submit to outdated moral standards designed to keep us cowed and frightened. I'm one of them. What's more important, though, is that we refuse to let the word sting, or draw distinctions between 'good' and 'bad' women.

Sexual liberation has been cut out and hammered down into sexual neoliberalism: rigid, suffocating conformity masquerading as freedom. Don't be fooled by the skin-mags and flesh-flashing music videos. We're in the middle of a sexual counter-revolution, and it starts with the ritual shaming of women and girls for daring to be creatures that lust.

TELL ME AGAIN ABOUT LIBERATION

In societies ravaged by the financial incompetence of rich men, it is the sexual incontinence of young women that is deemed the real danger to our children's futures. An epidemic of wanton slaggery is depicted, and little girls have to be protected from themselves, even as men on both sides of the Atlantic and the political spectrum queue up to justify rape.

Liberal and conservative lawmakers alike have come out in public to defend rapists, to excuse sexual violence as 'bad bedroom etiquette' or something less than 'legitimate rape', to explain that rape is inevitable, that the best way to protect oneself from it is to say 'no'. If that 'no' isn't respected, well, that's what you get for being born on the wrong side of the right chromosome.[5] We are told, again and again, that it is sexuality itself that is bad for women. In fact, what hurts women and girls is sexual control, just as it always has been – and the backlash is on.

Telling little girls to 'just say no' is official policy on sex education curriculum on several continents. But that does no good when it turns out that that 'no' won't always be respected. It's even less use in a sexual culture where 'no' is one of the most erotic things a woman can say. The fetishisation of female resistance – the erotics of 'no' – is ancient, but it is not immutable.

The ideal woman is fuckable, but never actually fucks. If she isn't a virgin she is, at least, perpetually refusing your advances; if she wants to 'catch' a man she must give every appearance of not wanting him, dropping his calls, not returning texts, playing 'hard to get'. Real men don't want women to want what they want; instead of a meeting of minds and squishy bits, sex is all about her submitting to his desires. Girls learn from their peers, from magazines and even from their mothers that they'll never get a boyfriend if they dare express desire, let alone lust. Doing so makes us objects of ridicule, clingy, needy, hysterical bitches who have been stupid enough to abandon the one power we're really allowed: the power to manipulate men with sexuality.

That's the one power women are really permitted, even if only a few of us, even if only for a small part of our lives, and only grudgingly. Of course it doesn't come for free – it comes with the constant threat of violence if we go too far, if we push him too much, if we send the wrong signals or have the audacity to change our minds. A woman who voluntarily abandons that power, a woman who is proud of her sex drive, who pursues men, who is predator rather than prey, who wants to meet her lovers as equals theoretically and horizontally, a woman like that will never be respected. Not when the emotional logic of neoliberalism still resists the idea that women are human beings with talents beyond prick-teasing and pregnancy.

More and more these days, sex looks like work. When the female orgasm was first discussed openly in the 1970s,[6] it was a revelation – it is now an obligation. If you can't make it, you have to fake it: produce pleasure, or pretend pleasure, doesn't matter, as long as you produce.

An orgasm is a bit like a smile: if you don't feel like it, you can fake it till you do. A woman without a smile on her face is a threat. Who hasn't been yelled at in the street – cheer up, love, it might never happen! – even when it already has? You look so much prettier when you smile. Smiling exercises all the right muscles in your face, it's practically exercise.

Did you know that when you smile, if you hold it for long enough, after a while you'll start to feel happy? Yes, I knew that, too – it's in all the magazines. Smiling is like fucking: if you'd rather not, maybe you should give it a try anyway, if your boss or your boyfriend would rather you did. Let's have no sulky faces. You'll get into it after a while. You'll learn to enjoy it. You'll learn.

Since the so-called 'sexual revolution' of the 1960s, women have more sex, but not freely, and not without fear of punishment that is social and sometimes physical. Dress like a slut and get raped; don't expect police protection if you engage in sex work or sleep around; break a man's heart and get battered. The 'cuckold's defence' for partner violence, whereby husbands whose wives had cheated on them were given lesser sentences for beating and even killing them, was taken off the statute books as late as 2009 in many countries, including Britain.[7]

The simple fact is that women do have sex, and lots of it, for reasons that are nothing to do with marriage or propriety. It's not just a few prostitutes or 'bad' women who fuck as if we already live in a world where we can't be punished for it; having sex with several partners before or outside long-term relationships has become, with the exception of strictly religious communities, the norm. 'Waiting until marriage' is now seen as unusual, a minority lifestyle choice, almost a perversion, which of course it is, and always was. Like any perversion, the 'purity before marriage' fetish is perfectly healthy in its proper place between private individuals, but as soon as it's enforced, it starts to stink of social control.

Sex by its nature is not bad for women. If the pursuit of pleasure remains a risky business for us it is because society makes it so, particularly if we are queer, or transsexual, or poor, or women of colour, or sex workers, or vulnerable. The social cost of actually having sex, rather than merely appearing to want to have it, is what damages women; sexual control, not sex itself, is what harms all of us.

BAD EDUCATION

September 2000. That time has come again. Last year's obligatory sex education class was run by the school nurse, a jolly middle-aged woman in a navy-blue shirt who owned a truly astonishing collection of full-frontal photographs of the most damply oozing sexually transmitted infections. This year, however, the nurse is sick. Her job has been given to a newly arrived languages teacher, Miss Green, owing to the notion that telling a roomful of sniggering, murder-eyed fourteen-year-olds everything they think they already know about fucking will burn all that youthful idealism right out of her.

We wait for Miss Green in the classroom like a pack of hunting dogs waiting for dinner. She comes in with a stack of videos and gives us an evil grin. An hour later half the boys are hiding their faces and all the girls are open-mouthed and angry. We have just watched information reels about how hard it is to get an abortion when you can't pay privately, and how you're forced to beg and cry and plead for basic autonomy over your own body.

It turns out that Miss Green of the mousy bob and unthreatening cardigan has an agenda. In one term of classes we learn a lot of things she technically isn't required to teach us, such as positions, painkillers and emergency contraception, including a trick with a shower nozzle you can do if a condom breaks before you run out for the morning-after pill, which Miss Green acts out in eye-popping detail. What Miss Green tells us is that we should not be frightened of our bodies. She tells us that the threat of pregnancy is only terrifying because of the ongoing assault on our reproductive choices.

When you are a teenage girl, absolutely the worst thing you can do is get pregnant. Pregnancy, if you're still in school, is synonymous with shameful life-ruinage, poverty and destitution, the doom of anyone silly and slutty enough to actually do all the things we're only meant to look like we want to. How precisely you are supposed to avoid this fate is a matter for debate. It's muddled by myth and sketchy sex education, skewed by shame and religious propaganda – there are a great many places in the nominally civilised world where telling young girls how to access contraception, much less giving them that access, is still against the law.[8] One thing, however, is made quite clear long before your tits come in and the bleeding starts: get pregnant and your life is over.

That simple fact of biological inequality – the fact that for women sex comes with the risk of pregnancy – is still the first and most important lesson young girls learn about why they are different to boys, why sex and love and life will always be different and difficult for us, why we have to be constantly on guard not to slip, not to shame ourselves or our families. Rather than teaching young girls about contraception and sexual health, we teach them shame. Rather than teaching young girls about pleasure, we teach them fear and self-hatred. And rather than teaching young boys about responsibility, we teach them suspicion and slut-shaming, teach them that sex is something they have to cheat and trick girls into giving up.

The fact that this narrative is insisted upon, despite the fact that we have the contraceptive technology to make it almost obsolete, is profoundly political.

When you are a teenage girl, all sorts of people suddenly start telling you what you can and can't do with your body. Your sexual and physical agency belongs to everyone apart from you. People suddenly have all sorts of opinions about how you look, what you wear, where you go and who you touch; men want to use you and sometimes abuse you for sex, and the magazines you read and the culture you consume confirms that the purpose of your body is to please men, whether or not you're at all interested in fucking them, and you probably shouldn't be, because you're a nice girl.

Aristotle, who was the sort of vicious misogynist that people have paid attention to for two thousand years, believed that women were incapable of higher reasoning because we are more animalistic than men, more bound to our bodies – women were bodies first before they were whole beings, and those bodies needed to be kept in line by men with muscle.[9] Two thousand years later, the same logic is at play at the highest levels of government. It is at play whenever lawmakers suggest that women should be forced to go to counselling before they can have an abortion.[10] It is at play whenever the state decides it knows better than women what our sexual autonomy should look like. It is at play when one in five women will be raped in her lifetime,[11] and the public conversation is stuck on how many of those women are liars.

It is no surprise that so many women and girls have what are delicately called 'control issues' around their bodies, from cutting and injuring their flesh to starving or stuffing themselves with food, compulsive exercise, or pathological, unhappy obsession over how we look and dress. Adolescence, for a woman, is the slow realisation that you are not considered as fully human as you hoped. You are a body first, and your body is not yours alone: whether or not you are attracted to men, men and boys will believe they have a claim on your body, and the state gets to decide what you're allowed to do with it afterwards.

A LOT OF KINKY FUCKERY

Things that Jean-Jacques Rousseau really liked included the philosophy of universal liberty, and having young ladies spank him into a frenzy. In *The Confessions*, he wrote: 'To fall at the feet of an imperious mistress, obey her mandates, or implore pardon, were for me the most exquisite enjoyments, and the more my blood was inflamed by the efforts of a lively imagination the more I acquired the appearance of a whining lover.'[12]

Like a great many wealthy, important men throughout history, Rousseau was a humiliation slut. He loved to have women boss him around in bed. He was also a flasher, and liked to moon unsuspecting ladies in the street and then prostrate himself for punishment. Nobody has ever suggested that this meant that the great enlightenment philosopher secretly wished men didn't run the world. In fact, Rousseau had some very specific things to say about women's place in the social order. 'Woman was specifically made to please man,' he wrote in *Emile*. 'If man ought to please her in turn, the necessity is less direct. His merit lies in his power . . . If woman is made to please and to be subjugated to man, she ought to make herself pleasing to him rather than to provoke him.'[13]

Kink has been part of the sexual menu for so long that it's hard to pretend anyone is shocked any more when it turns up on the table. The practice of male masochism, for example, has become almost idiomatic when one is discussing Wall Street workers, or the British aristocracy – despite Rousseau and de Sade, the French still refer to sadomasochism as '*le vice anglais*'. At no point, however, has anyone implied that men who want to be sexually dominated by women also want to be dominated by them socially and economically. Quite the opposite, if the long history of powerful men paying poor women to beat them up in backrooms is anything to go by. For women, though, the mainstreaming of kink – and particularly of sadomasochism – is supposed to prove that we're not as into all this liberation schtick as we might think.

In a cover story for *Newsweek* in 2012, columnist Katie Roiphe argued that the recent success of pop-porn bestseller *Fifty Shades of Grey* proves that even feminists secretly want to be shagged into submission by great, big, whip-wielding brutes. Not just in spite of our feminism, but because of our feminism. Roiphe claimed that modern women find 'the pressure of economic participation . . . exhausting' and that 'for some, the more theatrical fantasies of sexual surrender offer a release, a vacation, an escape from the dreariness and hard work of equality.'[14] This is the type of bullshit faux-feminism that the mainstream, woman-hating press just loves to pump out in order to provoke a reaction, propping up its ailing business model with the titillation of hate.

The first thing to note is that sexual submission is the acceptable face of female perversion: pliable, obedient and all about pleasing your man. Most of the available submissive fantasies that Roiphe and others have cited as part of a 'trend' of submission insist on their protagonists' initial unwillingness to be tied to enormous beds and rogered by wealthy professionals. In *Fifty Shades of Grey*, the protagonist only acquiesces to the kink because she wants to please her dominant lover. In *The Story of O* – which, although hardly part of a 'trend', having being written in the fifties, is still one of the only dirty books written for women that you can buy in respectable shops – 'O' agrees to be whipped and fucked by rich anonymous strangers to please her partner, Renee. These women may learn to love being spanked, but they certainly don't seek it out: they are passive, rather than just submissive.

In real life, men and women enjoy being bossed around in bed for lots of reasons – sometimes it might be about being punished, sometimes it might be about working out personal baggage, sometimes it might be about taking the break from all the responsibilities you have outside the bedroom, and sometimes it might just be about wanting someone else to do the work. And sometimes, yes, it might be about wanting to experience sex without having to take responsibility for your own desires – it's not as if we live in a culture where women who want to have sex are encouraged to have it in a shame-free way. Both *Fifty Shades of Grey* and *Twilight*, the teen series the adult erotic novel was based on, are fantasies of pursuit, of the responsibility for sexual agency being entirely in the hands of a man, who desires the point-of-view-protagonist completely.

In a culture where women who express sexual agency are punished, humiliated and threatened with real rather than ritualised violence, that sort of fantasy is entirely comprehensible. What is more significant is that submission – alongside, from time to time, sex work – is the only kind of female sexual 'unorthodoxy' that is currently deemed worthy of discussion, and it's an unorthodoxy trussed up tight in the bondage tape of patriarchal expectations. An unorthodoxy that happens to involve fantasies of being dominated by men. An unorthodoxy practised exclusively, if we go by the examples that fascinate the mainstream press, by women who are young and white and straight and middle-class and, most importantly, fucking fictional.

Fantasies about pretty young white women being controlled, hurt and dominated by men have always been the part of kink that nobody ever really had a problem with. During the crackdowns on the fetish and kink communities in the 1980s and early 1990s, submissive heterosexual women and their play partners were rarely targeted for prosecution. Today, when you think of 'fetish', many people think of Jean Paul Gaultier models strutting the runway in elegant leathers, and arty snaps of willowy girls doing Japanese rope bondage in low-lit loft apartments. You might not be quite so quick to picture middle-aged gay couples in matching latex, or enormous, hairy men with names like Nigel waddling around fetish clubs with joysticks up their bottoms and big grins on their faces, but kink has always been as much about them as it has been about the beautiful young girls, breakable or pretending to break others, who in real life tend to have less disposable income to spend on rubber.

Here are some non-standard sexual trends that editors at *Newsweek*, *Glamour* and *Cosmopolitan* are less keen to make headlines out of: poor women fucking. Black women fucking. Queer women fucking. Old women fucking. Fat women fucking; ugly women fucking; bossy, arrogant women fucking. Women who are dominant in bed. Women who like to penetrate men with big pink strap-ons. Women who want multiple sexual partners at once or in succession. Women who just want to go to bed early with a cup of tea, an Anna Span DVD and a spiked dildo the size of an eggplant. Here are some more: sex workers who want to be treated like workers, rather than social pariahs. Men who want to get fucked. Men who are gentle and submissive in bed. Men who don't enjoy penetrative sex. Men for whom sex is an overwhelming emotional experience. I guarantee you that all of these things go on, but any of them might actually destabilise for a second our cultural narrative of sex, gender and power, so none of them are allowed to be 'trends'.

In truth, there has never been anything controversial about the fantasy of female submission. These days, most of the 'mainstream' pornography readily available online involves some variation on the theme of outrages against young, prone, fuckable females. The rituals of whips, leather and safe-words are not part of the language of 'normal' porn, but otherwise the horny prospect of prone pretty girls having violent sex done to them and learning to love it is a dialect of desire everyone understands – so much so that lots of young men grow up knowing no other box to put their lust in. In Lena Dunham's *Girls*, the protagonist's useless hipster quasi-boyfriend spouts 'dirty talk' that Katie Roiphe identifies as specifically sado-masochistic – but actually, it could be lifted off the commentary on any 'vanilla' porn site. Check it out on RedTube.com if you don't believe me. Actually, don't. Actually, do.

Female sexual submission has never really been shocking. Right now, we are in the middle of a sexual counter-revolution. The backlash is on against even the limited amount of erotic freedom women have won over fifty years of hard campaigning: abortion and birth control are under attack, sexual health clinics are kitted out with bomb detectors and staffed by doctors who come to work wearing bullet-proof vests,[15] and a fully grown woman is denounced as a slut and a whore by male commentators across America for suggesting as part of a congressional hearing that yes, she may once or twice have had intercourse for pleasure rather than procreation.[16] And men who consider contraceptives morally wrong continue to be put forward as semi-serious contenders for leader of the free world.[17]

The sexual heresies that truly upset the pearl-clutchers of middle America have nothing to do with whips and chains. That's just faux-outrage, a bit of editorial baiting designed to upset feminists and titillate everyone else who likes to get cross and horny over the idea of dirty little girls tied up with tape.

No, what really gets social conservatives angry still happens not in swanky fetish clubs, but behind the closed doors of abortion clinics. It's women who want to be able to choose to terminate a pregnancy. Women who want to control their own fertility. Women who want sexual autonomy, which is what any attack on abortion rights is fundamentally about. Women who want to live independently or raise children without the help of men. Women who want sex on its own merit, whether it comes wrapped in black bondage rope or scattered with rose petals.

Female sexual autonomy itself is what's really unorthodox today. Agency and self-determination, the right to own our own desire – those are the kind of forbidden fantasies women across the world still pant over in private, unable to pronounce for fear of being slut-shamed. As Rousseau might put it: 'Whether the woman shares the man's desires or not, whether or not she is willing to satisfy them . . . the appearance of correct behaviour must be among women's duties.'[18]

OBJECTS OF DESIRE

Men are supposed to be desiring beings. That men and boys are constantly, aggressively up for it is rarely questioned, and those who have a more complicated relationship with erotic desire, those who would prefer to be seduced, those who are shy and unsure, those who would rather be fucked than do the fucking, those who would rather stay at home with a cup of tea and Skyrim and maybe talk dirty to a stranger on the Internet if she fancies it – those men and boys are not invited to speak of their desires. Sex is something men are supposed to want, and enjoy, and know instinctively how to do. For women and girls, sex is meant to be more like work, and that work is identified as our primary identity just as clearly as a male police officer or bank director is a cop or a capitalist before anything else, in this world where profession makes us.

Men have sex; women are sex. Being a woman, and being a woman whose role in life is to sexually attract, please and coddle men is still phrased as the primary occupation of every female, although some of us are still on strike.

For women living in a society where men rule, sexuality has always been work, and alienated work at that. You're expected to perform sex as a posture all the time, not to please yourself but to keep other people happy, and you'll get on just fine as long as you don't ever ask for power or pay. The men in our lives forget how to behave like lovers and instead behave like bosses, expecting a certain standard of performance while remaining terrified that we will one day realise our own power. The orgasm itself is work, something you have to produce in order to satisfy your partner, or the person behind the camera, if there's a difference. Your performance will be measured, tested, held up to a certain standard: you're not getting laid, you're getting graded.

To admit desire is to make a serious professional mistake: to own up to lust is to surrender 'erotic capital'. Women's only real power – still, always, in this nominally free world

– is supposed to be the power of 'no', even when that 'no' is worth so little in practice.

The frigid core of what we like to think of as modern, liberated sexuality does not reveal itself often. But there are clues, and one of them is that despite all those raunchy music videos the white-hanky brigade are perennially up in arms about, despite the porny pop-ups and airbrushed tits on every advert for soap and cereal, the generation that grew up in this notionally oversexed world still has next to no idea how to fuck, and we're not having it any more often than our parents did.

The phrase 'sexual objectification' is often used as shorthand for the welter of images of thin young white women prone and spread-eagled on every saleable surface, from newspapers to promotional panty-adverts. But what's wrong with objectification? Isn't that just what you do when you fancy someone? That rhetorical question, raised tirelessly by dumb choruses of big boys frightened that someone's going to take their spank bank away, deserves a little undressing.

Sexual objectification doesn't get oppressive until it is done consistently, and to a specific group of people, and with no regard whatsoever paid to their humanity. Then it ceases to be about desire and starts to be about control. Seeing another person as meat and fat and bone and nothing else gives you power over them, if only for an instant. Structural sexual objection of women draws that instant out into an entire matrix of hurt. It tells us that women are bodies first, idealised, subservient bodies, and men are not.

There is much discussion of what constantly having to look at those images does to girls' self-esteem, as if the problem would be solved if we could only make the poor little things feel better about their lives under the weaponised misogyny of neoliberalism. But boys have to see those pictures, too. What does that do to them?

For boys, sexual objectification of women is enforced long before sex itself is a realistic prospect. Ritual dehumanisation of women is part of how boys learn to bond, how they prove to one another that they are men. It's a sort of incantation against equality that starts at school and continues at work, in public space, when we walk the streets as adults. No matter how much we are told we ought to be flattered, dogwhistle sexual objectification of women and girls is chiefly performed by men for the benefit of other men.

Women's feelings don't really matter. That's the point.

Objectification itself isn't the problem. The problem is unequal objectification. And here, it's useful to remind ourselves of Caitlin Moran's litmus test for sexism, whereby if only women have to put up with a certain situation – say, seeing their gender reduced to oiled, half-naked, dead-looking stereotypes on every surface that'll take an advert before they've even had their cornflakes – then it's sexist.[19] When it comes to sexual objectification, the misogyny is in discrepancy. Objectification is oppressive when it erases every other form of desire apart from men's desire for women's commodified bodies.

The solution to this seems to be more boys in tight pants. Which is one of my favourite solutions to anything.

We can keep sexy pictures and still call a halt to the routine and oppressive sexual objectification of women and girls. We can keep naughty pin-ups, just so long as we provide them for people who aren't straight men. If the Internet has taught us one thing, it's that all kinds of people like to get their kit off for money and attention. Objectification can be mutual. It can be fun. It can even be freeing. But right now, for most of us, and particularly for women, sexual objection and sexual freedom are painfully different things.

My age group was among the first to grow up with hardcore pornography as a substitute for the plain sex education most of us were still denied. Shagging both within and outside your own cohort gives the lie to the idea that, behind closed zippers, young people are any better informed about sex than their parents. Just because you know what goes where doesn't mean you can get it in, or even that you do on a regular basis.

This apparent contradiction has gone unremarked, in the main because of the centuries-old overlap between those who complain loudest about the depravity of the young and those who suspect that the selfish, wanton and almost certainly infected youth of today are having not just more sex than they ever did, but more sex than anyone has ever had, in the history of the human race, ever. The fact that a recent study showed teenagers in 2012 were actually having less sex than teens did ten years ago[20] does not fit the narrative about a slow slide into erotic Armageddon, in part because nobody in their thirties can seriously contemplate the possibility that the youth of today are getting it less than they did.

It is possible to stand against censorship and still acknowledge that porn is a problem for men right now. It captivates them, because that's what it's designed to do, but it distresses them, too, and there needs to be an honest discussion about what porn does that goes beyond simple, impractical demands to ban all tits on film for ever. The script that young men in particular have been handed to learn about fucking from presents as normal a highly ritualised, aggressive heterosexuality played out by professionals who have to work hard to be good at what they do. It requires training, effort, and not a small amount of special equipment. There are people offstage making sure the lighting works and the talent stays hard.

The great genius of commercial sexuality has been to give the impression that this society is one of unprecedented erotic freedom while maintaining the impression that sex is almost always something violent and disgusting that men do to women. Hence the ubiquity of that pernicious little word 'sexualisation', which is used to describe everything from teeny push-up bras to music videos where the latest teen starlet to come off the Disney channel prances about in hotpants. Women should never be sexual: sex is something that is done to us, preferably as late and as infrequently as possible. At a certain age, we are 'sexualised', and then that's it. There's no going back. We are ruined, doomed to abject, knicker-dropping harlotry, and nobody will ever love us.

Sex is still phrased as violence, and rape as a logical extreme of that violence. The sex drive is understood as entirely male; women who pursue or demand sex are masculine and unnatural. So toxic and unstoppable is men's sex-hunger that women must be appointed guardians of it – if they provoke men's desire, if they dress in short skirts or low-cut tops, they have only themselves to blame if they get raped or assaulted.

The notion that fucking is something disgusting men do to women, and women who let them do it are somehow abject, remains scored in our sexual psyche, for all our claims to liberation. The received wisdom, duly transmitted in urban legend and the more vapid bedroom-advice sections of women's magazines, is that men are actually turned off by sexual forwardness – the more straight women who are not numb between the legs pursue the thing we want, the less likely we are to get it. 'She can't be too flirty – I have to chase her'; 'I want her to play innocent'; 'I like to be in control'. That's the type of talk that makes any sensible slut cross her legs at the anticipation of frustration now or in the future, when that pretty boy has finally opened up to you enough to make you an object of his most private self-loathing.

Teaching men self-disgust is crucial to maintaining the architecture of modern misogyny. If sex weren't dirty and degrading, there would be less reason to loathe women for letting you do it to them, no matter how much you want to. How could you possibly respect a creature who lets you take out your baser instincts on them, who even professed to enjoy it? How could you take seriously a person who shamed themselves in such a way? Women's dignity is impossible when the only thing worse than being an object and instrument of men's sexual shame is not being one.

UNPORNIFICATION

An incredible thing has happened. We live in an age of boundless information. Kids today are able to know more, much more, than any generation that has come before them. I'm writing this paragraph, for example, on a device no bigger than my open hand through which I can access, with a couple of finger-swipes, more data than my immediate ancestors ever conceived of in their days of hoarding books in island poverty, although I mainly use it to look at smutty webcomics and find my way to the pub. And yet, with all this hyperabundance of information, with all of these learning tools at our disposal, we have somehow managed to raise yet another generation that remains as ignorant and confused as ever about that most intimate of mysteries, human sexuality. How did this happen?

It happened because adults in this culture persist in seeing their own sexuality as monstrous, as terrifying and compelling and disgusting, rather than as a normal part of human development. It happened because we are unable to provide decent, adequate sex education in schools, or alternative models for sexuality beyond the sterile, the sexist and the crashingly heteronormative. If sex were food, we'd be unable to move for takeaways and fast food joints, living lives where the only nourishment offered or advertised was cystic chicken nuggets pumped full of MSG and aerated factory-line hamburgers that don't have the decency to decay even if you leave them on a windowsill for a week – and then wondering why everybody was still so hungry all the time. Of course, there are times when all you want is a double cheeseburger drowned in barbecue sauce, but if you try to live on it, you get sick, and bored, and drained of energy; you have to eat more and more of the stuff to feel satisfied, but somehow you never really do, because what your brain and body need aren't what your gut is being instructed to want.

The impression given by most industrially produced porn and its imitators, the one thing that most current mainstream pornography shares with the sexual script of advertising and the mantra of women's magazines, is the insistence that sex, like every other kind of alienated labour, is serious business. No fuck-ups are allowed – if you're not an expert from the get-go you'll surely find yourself replaced with someone cuter and more exploitable. There can be no giggling, no mistakes, no fanny farts, no awkward squeaking sounds when bodies rub together. Bodies should work more like machines, machines that don't get their feet caught in their pants or drop their stockings on the lit candle they thought would be romantic so a small fire starts. If an advert for organ donation comes on your Spotify shuffle playlist in the crucial thirty seconds, you mustn't laugh. That would be unprofessional.

In fact, if there's one thing pro-porn actors can teach the rest of us amateurs, it's the difference between the type of sex you have because it looks good and the kind you have because it feels good. In between takes of the former a lot of fumbling around and logistical discussion takes place. The porn actors I lived with when I first started writing seemed to spend most of their time giggling as they worked out what they could put on expense accounts.

The New Jersey Porn Xpo is in the middle of concrete shopping-mall hell and there isn't a single stall that can sell you an orgasm, although they give it a damn good try. The bored girl running the bucking bronco booth, a fairground ride in the manner of a rodeo bull shaped like an enormous squat phallus, seems mildly annoyed that nobody wants to ride her giant dick. In the midst of all this extravagance, the wild electric dong is turned off at the wall. The booth girl, draped over the saddle, closes her eyes.

Stoya, the porn star of the moment, is at her stall signing DVDs and fleshlights – custom moulds of her vagina that only a few porn stars are asked to sit for, quite literally. A queue of men trails down the aisle to speak to her, transfixed and shuffling as they might in the presence of royalty. Most are stammering, shy; some engage her in conversation about how she changed their life, their wives don't know they watch her films, but she really seems to enjoy it so it's all right, isn't it? A few of them are young, most are middle-aged, a small number are as pushy as they can get away with in a venue with security on hand to watch out for the girls. Stoya is a consummate professional. 'No one has ever said to me at a porn convention, "I fucked the shit out of your fleshlight pussy like a dirty whore!" Nobody's been downright nasty. Walking out on the street, though, where people have no idea who you are, dudes will tell you – "Man, I'd fuck that pussy." Bleurgh. That's when men yell at you. When you're in sneakers, when you haven't showered in three days. Six days. Whatever.'

Stoya tosses on a floor-length white coat, slings her wondrous bag of vaginas over one shoulder and heads out for a smoke. I join her. The air in the car park smells of nicotine and warm tarmac, but it seems surprisingly fresh in its upfront unhealthiness. Indoors is deodorised, and that, I realise, is what's been bugging me all along: I expect sex to smell. I expect an enormous hall full of sex to smell of something other than rubber and cleaning fluid. There is nothing organic here. Just hard-working people and the punters who pay their wages. The lingerie turns out to be tax-deductible, and I wonder briefly if I'm in the wrong job, but only briefly, as I have neither the stamina nor the charisma to be pleasant to everyone in the way that Stoya has to at gigs like these.

Stoya is not the first feminist porn star I've known, although a great number of the 'professional' women's liberation workers I've met still choose to pretend that feminist sex workers don't exist, like tooth fairies, or gay republicans. I should stress that I have never sold sex myself, mainly because I was advised against it by kind friends in the industry who suggested that my total lack of emotional boundaries and love of horrible grey knickers meant I should possibly stick to the day-job. But I am part of a community that includes many sex workers, many of my friends and lovers have sold and continue to sell sexual services, and when I am asked to speak about sex work as if my possession of lady parts and a public platform mean I know everything about sexual commodification it is those people I turn to.

Modern feminism lumbers under an uncomfortable inheritance from the women's activism of the 1980s that stressed sex work as damaging on point of principle. Stoya's feminist mother 'was not there on the day that the women threw the bras into the trashcans outside the Miss America pageant, but she ran with that crew. She was one of the bodies out there on the streets, holding signs. And that's wonderful,' she tells me, three days after the porn convention, in a small hipster cafe where every bearded laptop-scrabbler is sneaking surreptitious looks of longing at our table.

'My mother's view of the word that she imparted to me was: you're a person. You have a vagina, but you're a person first, you can do anything you want. But when I said I wanted to take ballet classes, you could see her gritting her teeth. She tried very hard to stick to what she'd said. But then there were performances, make-up, and she had her own ideas about how women ought to be. She had physically put herself at risk to open up women's rights!

'Some ladies have a chip on their shoulder [about sex work]. I respect that chip. But while that chip was probably necessary to get us to the point we are now, it's a prejudice. I'm immensely grateful that we're now at the place where I can have that choice, where I want to wear high heels, and make-up. I want to do pretty things. I want to sell my body professionally.' Stoya's mother remains uncomfortable with her decision to do porn. Her granny, however, is perfectly happy, and even allows Stoya to use her name as a professional pseudonym.

When a lot of feminists say they hate pornography and prostitution, what they mean is that they hate the transactional nature of sex, the patriarchal equation whereby every party remains convinced they're the one getting screwed: he pays her and she services him. In this equation, sex is work like anything else women do, low-paid or unpaid but work nonetheless, and approaching it for its own sake is frowned upon. What on earth would that get you, except laid, and what decent woman really wants that? Rich women who don't give a damn about exploitation in any other industry are moved by the plight of prostitutes. They alone are truly abject and must be rescued from their sinful way of life even if there's no alternative but begging. Surely begging is better, working twelve hours a day in a sweatshop is better, anything is better than fucking for money, because everyone knows that work is good for you and sex is bad for women. And so making sex work legal can't possibly happen – even if it saves lives, keeps prostitutes safe from the threat of arrest and imprisonment, and makes it easier for them. What kind of message would that send to children?

Using the phrase 'sex work' rather than 'prostitution', something many sex workers insist upon, reframes the debate. Instead of asking what it is about sex that is so bad for women, we can start asking what it is about work that's bad for everyone. That's a dangerous question. To argue that sex work is a job 'like any other' is not to argue that it is benign, on the contrary. Most jobs are awful, and the fact that some sex workers would rather not do what they do for a living implies nothing more than that: the gas-station attendant and the shop girl would probably also rather not have to do what they do all day, although they are obliged to put a smile on it and insist that they love their work.

And yet we continue to be told that there is something in particular about prostitution that threatens women – not just the women who do it, but all women. If a woman or girl is selling sexual services somewhere in the world, the overall cost of women's consent will be depreciated, and we all know that the power to refuse or permit intercourse is still our greatest asset. If withholding sexual consent is still many women's only way of bargaining for better conditions, in marriage, in relationships or in the family, then it's easy to see how sex workers might be undermining that bargaining power – as might any woman who gives it up too easily, for money or for pleasure. As long as we accept a world where sexual consent is still women's biggest bargaining chip, sex workers will suffer for our sins.

We cannot know what sex work is really like, or how prostitutes really suffer, the refrain goes, because how could they tell us? In fact, since the Internet made anonymous, self-published accounts of sex work feasible on a mass scale, hookers and strippers and porn stars and pro-dommes have been telling us just that, in their tens of thousands. When abolitionists can no longer pretend that sex workers are not speaking, the standard claim is that they have been so abused and traumatised by the work they do that their ideas do not matter and should not be respected. In other contexts, feminism is supposed to be about listening to women who have been abused and asking what they need, rather than telling them they're brainwashed whores with no idea what's good for them.

The idea of sex workers with agency, with real power over their working conditions and legal rights, upsets a lot of people for a lot of different reasons. For social conservatives, it's a threat to family life and public morals; for misogynists, it gives women more power to formalise the means by which they have exploited men for years, dragging them by the dicks while they empty their wallets without fear of violent punishment or social shame: unthinkable. If a woman is to earn real money from sex she must also know that it's the worst thing she can possibly do, that she's a filthy slut not worthy of the rights other workers once demanded. And the last group campaigning against the legalisation of prostitution are feminists.

The feminist sex wars are far less exciting than they sound.

They take place largely in draughty meeting rooms where people shout at each other until the buses stop running about whether prostitution is simply transactional rape.

Sex work isn't stigmatised because it is dangerous, it is dangerous because it is stigmatised, and that social stigma, that system of punishing and excluding sex workers from the brightly lit world of good, pure women who would never actually cash in on the erotic capital that is supposed to be our only power, is still with us.

SINGLE MUMS AND SCAPEGOATS

Alongside sex workers, the most hated character in the shadow-play of modern sexual prejudice is the single mother.[21] The millions of women raising children without a co-parent are spoken of in the same terms as beggars and thieves: they are a drain on the state, the scourge of hard-working taxpayers who must forfeit the proceeds of 'real' work to pay for the maintenance of these 'broken homes'. The charity Gingerbread estimates that nine in ten single parents are mothers;[22] many of these mothers are not raising children alone by choice, but because their primary relationships have ended or broken down, and it is significant that single mothers often feel obliged to insist, before asking for the means of survival, that they did at least try to be good. They tried to be good wives, to keep a family together. Single fathers, by contrast, are lauded as heroes, gamely raising children without the help of the wicked women who have abandoned their natural role.

In the single mother, contemporary slut-shaming and class

prejudice find their perfect scapegoat. The term 'fallen woman' is now considered archaic, but the mythology persists: women bring shame on themselves by lapsing from the pedestal of perfect neoliberal womanhood, the walking CV in stilettos who juggles the husband, child and corporate job with effortless ease.

Single mothers are not just sluts, they're bad entrepreneurs, lazy workers, dissident subjects who have failed to supply the demands of capitalist patriarchy and now demand that the rest of us pay for it. In the United States, there is no male equivalent for the term 'welfare queen'. Having a child alone and asking for support with raising that child – from her community, her family or the state – is considered uniquely selfish.

The logic of neoliberal gender politics insists that no woman is poor or struggling because of structural inequality, but because of her own choices. The single mother, like the prostitute, must have made bad choices, or shameful, dirty choices, that have left her destitute. She is unworthy of sympathy, much less assistance. She has failed to deploy her erotic capital wisely. Her child is a permanent reminder of those poor choices. The slut-shaming and social punishment of single mothers and their children gives the lie to modern ideas of sexual liberation – much less of reproductive freedom.

But it's not just single mothers who are shamed for daring to spawn: motherhood itself is now tacitly considered a selfish, dirty choice, a species of reproductive incontinence.

Girls who wish or are expected to attain social mobility are encouraged to delay childbearing. Campaigners against teenage pregnancy remind young women in no uncertain terms that having a child before they've staked out a metaphorical spot in the corner office will 'ruin your life' – one is never supposed to question why. Having children is something poor girls do, something foolish girls do: as evidence, we are reminded that poverty is a strong predictor of teenage pregnancy. Once you start breeding, it's game over, girl. Unless you're very rich or very lucky, your chances of a fulfilling life on its own terms just got suckered. And yet those of us who were raised female in or after the 1980s were told, in ominous tones, that we would one day 'want kids', in the manner in which you might be informed that you have a chronic illness which will one day leave you crippled.

The morality tale of our age is the poor mother with many children. These women are demonised as grossly fecund, perpetually pushing pramfuls of squalling brats down dingy estate streets. Their fertility and their poverty form a cage of disgrace that they might have escaped had they only kept their legs shut and their feet on the career ladder. Reality television shows across the West invite viewers to gawp at the gall of the underclass in continuing to breed.[23]

Motherhood may have been relegated to a species of reproductive deviance, but that is not to say that women are permitted to live as if their fertility is not fundamental to their being. On the contrary: women's potential fertility is still given as an excuse for not hiring or promoting female employees whether or not they plan, or indeed are able, to have children. We can expect to be questioned, at any job interview, about whether we plan to have kids, thus costing the state or our bosses valuable money that might have been spent training and hiring a man.

Fathers, of course, are nowhere in this equation. It is assumed that most men, given the choice, would want to escape the onerous duties of parenthood. Those who do take an active role in parenting are afforded secular sainthood although they cannot expect any practical support from their bosses or from the state in the form of paternity leave. The raising and production of the next generation – the means of reproduction – are still very much the domain of women, and they are resented for it.

The perfect worker maintains the appearance of sterility: she looks fuckable, but never actually fucks, much less reproduces, and God forbid she arrive at the front desk with baby food dried on her lapels. If she has responsibilities outside the 'workplace' she is expected to manage them in private. Raising and bearing children is not considered work – you don't get paid for it, so how could it be?

Women are selfish if we have children and selfish if we don't: we are expected to anticipate the stretching of our energies between our gross physical fecundity which will inevitably curtail our own chances and the demands of the workplace. We will be stretched, overtaxed and judged whatever we choose, and that's just the way the world works. That's just what the market demands. The anxieties that this produces are the perfect formula: panicked workers who are constantly juggling responsibilities do not tend to join unions or go on strikes, and they will generally accept whatever privations are foisted upon them, only too happy to please. The only mothers who are celebrated for the work they do are those who are somehow able to combine the labour of motherhood with 'wealth creation' – that is, with maintaining well-paid, 'high-flying' employment, typically in the financial sector.

Having children does not just interrupt work: it is anti-work. Women, because motherhood is still assumed to be in their nature, are inherently anti-work, and must atone for it by toiling harder and longer, in less secure and less well-paid positions than those employees who might not, at any point, drop a baby. Our sexual bodies are still the source of original sin, except the transgression is not now against religious morality, but against the market.

THE MEANS OF REPRODUCTION

It's not big and it's not clever and I shouldn't do it because it's a cheap shot. But here I am again, on a street corner in Dublin, flirting with a pro-lifer. He's twenty-one and a committed Catholic and his name is Dennis and he's trying to explain to me why abortion is sinful, and there's a rising flush in his face as I ask him if he's got any comment on what the hell a girl is supposed to do when contraception fails, as it sometimes does.

'There's obvious steps she can take to not have a child,' he tells me.

Like what?

'Well, for example, abstinence,' says Dennis.

Can he tell me more? I draw my tongue across my teeth and do that thing you can do with a heavy backpack where you shift it around your shoulders so it momentarily pushes your tits up and forward. Dennis starts to blush despite the cold. 'Purity before marriage,' he explains.

Really, Dennis, I'm fascinated – tell me all about purity before marriage.

Around the corner, young women with pamphlets calling for abortion to be legalised are being sworn at in the street. It's a freezing January day, and they only have each other. One of them tells me that she had to travel to England, where abortion is still legal, taking a flight alone and paying money she could ill afford to have a procedure that would see her thrown out of the house and shamed at work if she identified herself. Over the past five decades 150,000 Irish women and girls have done the same, and most have never spoken of it.[24] I fight the desire to put away the recorder and give her a hug, or all my strength, or a world that doesn't hate women. Instead, I give her some chocolate from my pocket. It is madly insufficient.

In Ireland, abortion is illegal. In many parts of the nominally developed world, including a great many American states, safe, legal termination of pregnancy is either outlawed or functionally illegal,[25] the centre of a matrix of rage and shame directed at desperate, anonymous women who cannot speak out for fear of violent reprisals.

If a woman didn't want to have sex, though, abortion suddenly becomes okay. Most states and nations with laws restricting abortion to the point of a ban make exceptions for rape and incest.[26] Any qualms about the feelings of the nugget of cells forming in the uterus are instantly, magically less important than a woman's autonomy if she was raped or subjected to incest, because a woman who really, truly didn't want to have sex is a good woman and shouldn't be punished for it, whereas bad women who consent to sex, who might even actually enjoy it, deserve to suffer the consequences.

The backlash against abortion access and contraceptive

availability is a sexist backlash, rooted in fear of female autonomy and hatred of women's sexuality. It is phrased, of course, as concern for women. Almost every effort to control women's sexuality is, on the understanding that sex is bad for us and we're essentially vapid, thoughtless creatures who cannot be trusted with control over our own bodies.

The religious and conservative right, especially in the United States and in majority Catholic countries, continues to claim that abortion and contraception are sinful,[27] to which the obvious retort is that God also created smallpox, polio and erectile dysfunction, but that hasn't stopped medical science from helping us lead longer and more exciting lives without them. Increasingly, however, we are told that pregnancy termination and birth control are somehow psychologically damaging to women – that we can't cope with all this freedom, that the maternal impulse rebels, that abortion is so psychologically damaging that women should be forbidden access to it.[28] Being at the mercy of one's biology, however, being forced to give birth to a child against one's will and raise it in poverty or give it away – these things are deemed psychologically healthy. The wealthy men and religious zealots who still largely make the laws that control women's access to reproductive healthcare will never need abortions, but as men, they are clearly best placed to decide what's good for women in nominally democratic countries.

It is stunning, however, how fast this language of concern mutates into slut-shaming and gross misogyny. In America, women who admit in public to using contraception, like law student Sandra Fluke, who spoke up in favour of hormonal birth control at an all-male senate hearing in 2012, are called sluts and harpies, ugly whores. Liberals, meanwhile, still lack the guts to make a case for why women should be permitted full adult sexual agency to the greatest extent that modern technology allows. Instead, they echo the language of conservatives to the effect that abortions are universally tragic and the reason we need contraception is to protect good women – mothers, especially mothers concerned for the well-being of existing children, or women with chronic hormonal illnesses – not to indulge bad women who merely want the kind of sexual autonomy men have always enjoyed.

The 'sexual revolution' of the 1960s and 1970s was supposed to be about liberating women from the privations of biology; so far, it has ended up being about releasing men from the responsibilities of domesticity. Setting society free from the imperative to marry and raise children with one's legally bonded life partner is, of course, a net gain for everyone – but something deeper has been lost. This is why, for the past twenty years, mainstream feminist conversation has been dominated by debate over whether a woman can have 'it all' – where 'it all' means taking care of her husband, children and boss at once. The question of why she should ever want to has never been adequately explained.

Sexual inequality is the fundamental basis of gender inequality, the biological logic by which one sex is kept subservient, to some degree, to the other. Even when women do not wish or are physically unable to conceive and carry children, they are obliged to submit to a social schedule set out to control the agency of those who are. The principle that sex is without consequences for men but dangerous for women because it is associated with the risk of pregnancy is a difficult principle for some people to let go of. It is women's job to resist men's advances for as long as possible and then to carry the burden of those advances; women should have sex done to us, never take control of it ourselves. There is no reason why this should be the case.

For several generations, we have had the medical technology to confine sex-class segregation to history: to make women truly the equals of men, who can have intercourse and engage with the opposite sex without fear of unwanted pregnancy, social stigma and painful death. The technological advances concerned are hormonal and physical contraception and safe medical abortion, both of which are an occasionally painful and traumatic hassle for women who make use of them, but far less painful and traumatic than being obliged to carry a growing foetus for nine months and then push it out through your pelvis.

The technology of sexual and reproductive liberation should have changed the world for women far more than it has. The reason that the relative reliability of condoms, hormonal contraception, emergency contraception and medical abortion is so threatening to men is that it alters the material basis of women's oppression.

As the basis of biological inequality began to be eroded by contraceptive technology and reproductive healthcare, a frantic backlash began – both against the technology and against the sexual freedom it enabled. Not only was the use of condoms and the Pill unnatural, not only was abortion a sin against God and man, any woman who would make use of such advances was clearly a soulless harlot who should be ashamed of herself. Never mind that most sexually active women and girls use contraception, and one-third of us will have an abortion at some point in our lives. The backlash against women's sexual autonomy is a backlash against everyone's sexual freedom, male and female, gay and straight.

Technological advances are meant to benefit humanity, but the notion that women and queer people are fully human seems yet to occur to a worrying proportion of lawmakers. Where women are permitted access to contraception and abortion, that access can't be made easy – we must never forget that our limited sexual freedom is the gift of powerful men, who can take it away again if we don't behave. We cannot fight this backlash by being polite. In a culture that wants us cowed and afraid, women and girls must weaponise our shamelessness.

WHAT WE TALK ABOUT WHEN WE TALK ABOUT RAPE CULTURE

Structural sexism does not always come from a place of hate. The clearest example of this is the conversation about date-rape, drugs and drinking.

At the time of writing, the debate is raging over whether or not a woman ever has a responsibility to 'protect' herself from rape. A great many people, too many to name and shame, have spent time and energy pleading with young women in particular to stop drinking and taking drugs, to stop giving the 'wrong' signals to men, to be careful never to walk down strange streets alone. Often, the people making these pleas are good-hearted. They want young girls and women to be as safe as possible. It is for our own good that girls are encouraged never to let down our guard.

But that's the whole problem.

Down the centuries, women and girls have been told not to do all sorts of things 'for our own good'. We have been told not to go to work, not to read too much, not to go to school or to university because it would be damaging for us; we are still told not to go out alone, enjoy our sexuality or speak our minds in public because that might provoke violent retribution from the dwindling number of men who believe that women should be silent sexual commodities and nothing else. In Saudi Arabia, the reason given for preventing women from driving is that it might damage their ovaries. If women as a class had always listened to everyone telling us to place limits on ourselves for our own safety, we would all still be stuck in the kitchen.

Right now, a few bouts of irresponsible drinking are practically a rite of passage in many nations – and the rights and wrongs of that state of affairs are another debate entirely.

Arguing over whether or not it is a woman's 'responsibility' to protect herself from rape prevents us from discussing the real issue, which is when precisely society is going to start placing the blame for rape on the men who commit rape, the criminal justice system which refuses to take it seriously, and the wider culture of silence and shame which allows men and boys to continue raping women, girls and other men with relative impunity.

Telling young women that we are not allowed to make the same mistakes, have the same fun or take the same risks that young men do – risks like getting drunk, going out adventuring or travelling alone – may offer us some protection from predators in the short term. But in the long term it just gives those predators more power. It gives them the power to control women's behaviour, to keep us fearful, and to make sure we cannot have fun and take risks without the threat of sexual violence. That's what rape culture is all about, and rape culture is strengthened every time we tell young women to drink less or risk sexual assault.

When our great-grandparents' generation urged their daughters to marry young or face social purgatory they thought they were doing so in their best interests. A hundred years later, when we tell our friends and children and younger sisters not to stay out late, not to walk in certain areas of the city after dark, and not to go out and get hammered in Hastings, we are thinking the same thing. We tell women and girls these things, not always because we secretly hate them, but because we care about them, we want to protect them, individually, from a world that we know isn't as equal as we sometimes pretend.

This is what we are fighting when we fight rape culture, not just career misogynists spreading their bile over the airwaves like so much tacky mucus, but the quiet voice inside us that whispers, 'Not so fast.' The voice that tells us that if only we stay home and keep our legs closed and our eyes lowered we'll be safe.

Unfortunately, however, rape culture gets you coming and going. It is precisely about fear, about creating a culture where women are afraid to participate in public life as men do. A life lived in fear of sexual violence, a life where you cannot take the risks that men take without anticipating physical attack or, worse still, being attacked and then blamed for it, is not a life lived freely. It isn't even going to protect you or those you love: in a recent study, more than half of all rape victims in the United States reported being raped by an intimate partner, a boyfriend, husband or lover.[29] Most rapists are known to and trusted by the person they assault. Behaving 'responsibly' is not, ultimately, any protection against sexual violence.

Here's what is understood when a senior police officer broadcasts a public message warning women not to do something they'll 'regret' on a night out: this is the way the world is.[30] We are meant to understand that rape and sexual assault are facts of life and, much as we may disapprove, much as we may want to see rapists brought to justice, there is nothing we can do to combat structural violence. That kind of rape myth is damaging enough when it comes from a friend or a parent. It's far more harmful when it comes from law enforcement, or from an official government source.

Here's what we must begin to say to today's young women, all over the world. Rape does not have to be a fact of life. It is not your responsibility to be cautious, to restrict yourself, to be quieter and better behaved so that men don't rape you. If you choose to live your life in fear of male violence, nobody will think any less of you – the fear is pertinent and legitimate, and sometimes there are grave consequences for women who talk too loudly and flirt too much and take too many risks. But here's the thing: there are also consequences for those who don't.

To live in rape culture is to balance the possibility of being at less risk of sexual violence if you dress conservatively, don't go out and have fun, don't travel alone and don't ever upset your partner against the certainty that you will live a smaller, sadder life. It is not about protecting women. It is about controlling women.

An enormous change in consciousness is taking place around consent, and it threatens to change everything. At some point between 2008 and 2014, the collective understanding of what rape and abuse are, and what they ought to be, changed for ever. At some point we began to talk, not just privately, cowedly, but in numbers too big to ignore, about the reality of sexual violence and child abuse, about how victims are silenced. Survivors of rape and abuse and their loved ones had always known this toxic truth, but we were forced to hold it close to ourselves where it could fester and eat us from within. A great many women you know have intimate experience of this. We just didn't talk about it in quite this way before.

Something has changed. A change in the way we communicate and interact has allowed people who have traditionally been isolated – say, victims of rape and child abuse – to speak out, to share their stories without mediation, to make the structures of power and violence we have always known were there suddenly visible, a thing that can be challenged.

There are people out there, not all of them men, who believe that a conspiracy is going on. When I speak to them as a reporter, they tell me that women lie about rape, now more than ever. They lie to damage men and 'destroy their lives'. This is despite the fact that the fraud rate for rape remains as low as ever, and despite the fact that popular culture is groaning with powerful men who have been accused of sexual abuse whose lives remain distinctly undestroyed. Men like boxer Mike Tyson, or singer R. Kelly, or filmmaker Woody Allen. Women and children who bring those accusations, however, risk their relationships, their reputation, their safety. Anonymity in the press is no protection against the rejection of family, friends and workmates. We have created a culture and a legal system which punishes those who seek justice so badly that those who do come forward are assumed to have some ulterior motive.

Rape and abuse are the only crimes where, in the words of the seventeenth-century legal scholar Lord Matthew Hale, 'it is the victim, not the defendant, who is on trial'. They are crimes that are hard to prove 'beyond reasonable doubt' in a court of law, because it's a case of 'he said, she said'. Nobody can really know, and so naturally we must assume that he is innocent and she is lying, because that's what women do. The trouble is that in this society, 'he said' is almost always more credible than 'she said', unless she is white and he is not.

The rule of law cannot be relied upon when it routinely fails victims of abuse. That is not the end of the conversation. The law courts aren't the only place where the nature of sexual power, of what men may and may not do to women, children and other men with impunity, is played out. No magistrate can ensure that a young girl like Missouri teenager Daisy Coleman, who came forward last year to describe how she was raped by classmates at a party, is not hounded out of town, along with her family, until she makes attempts on her own life.

Rape culture means more than a culture in which rape is

routine. Rape culture involves the systematic suspicion and dismissal of victims. In order to preserve rape culture, society at large has to believe two different things at once: that women and children lie about rape, and that they should also behave as if rape will be the result if they get into a strange car, walk down a strange street, or wear a sexy outfit, and if it happens, it's their own fault.

This paradox involves significant mental gymnastics. But as more and more people come forward with accusations, as the pattern of historical and ongoing abuse of power becomes harder to ignore, the paradox gets harder to maintain. We are faced with two alternatives: either women and children are lying about rape on a massive scale, or rape and sexual abuse are endemic in this society, and have been for centuries. Facing up to the reality of the latter is a painful prospect.

If we were truly to accept the enormity of rape culture, if we were to understand what it actually means that one in five girls and one in ten boys are sexually abused, it will not just be painful. It will force our culture to reimagine itself in a way that is uncomfortable even to contemplate. As Jessica Valenti writes at the *Nation*, 'It will mean rethinking institutions and families and power dynamics and the way we interact with each other every day.'[31] It will mean looking with new eyes at our most revered icons, our social groups, our friends and relatives. It will involve hard, difficult work. It will change everything. And it has already begun.

The sexual counter-revolution is on, and it's urgent, and it is about control. It gets excited with ritual sexual objectification of women, sweats over silencing critics of rape culture, and works itself into a frenzy over contraception, abortion and reproductive freedom. We have been lied to. If women and queer people still shackle our desires in shame and silence, we are not as liberated as we think. If sexual freedom is the sole domain of straight men and boys, not one of us is truly free.

We have the technology to liberate women and girls from the shackles of biology. What we do not have, yet, after over a century of fighting for it, is the collective will to make that liberation real.

The backlash against real sexual freedom – the radical emancipation of pleasure from power – is powerful and sustained. As all human affect collapses into the logic of the market, it is not just sex which has become a commodity, it is intimacy itself.

Real sexual empowerment is not just about the fun stuff. It's not just about dildos and lacy thongs and pole-dancing classes. It's about abortion rights. It's about contraception. It's about ending rape culture. It's about creating a world where pleasure and self-expression does not have to be offset with fear of violence and unwanted pregnancy.

We have the technological means to make that kind of sexual freedom a liveable possibility for billions of people. The mechanisms of shame are as important to neoliberal sexual ideology as the illusion of choice. In theory, sex does not need to cost more for cis women than it does for anyone else, in terms of fear of pregnancy, disease or social shame. The fact that it still does is an assault on the sexual liberty and personhood of every human being.

We have been sold a single idea of what sexual freedom is,

and it still looks a great deal like serving a restricted menu of male fantasy, sliced and packaged for uncomplicated consumption. In this grim meat-packing-factory of identikit heterosexuality, female flesh and female desire are treated as scarce natural resources. Like any other scarce natural resource, they are there to be mined and exploited. Pleasure is stripped, commodified and sold back to us. We are not allowed to own our own desire. We are not permitted to feel in charge of our own bodies.

The relaxation of moral standards in the age of contraception and antibiotics has not ended the enclosure of female sexuality. It has not returned the common ground of pleasure, adventure and desire to human beings of every gender. It has merely built a theme-park on the common ground and invited straight men weary from the indignities to buy a ticket and come and play.

There are still those of us who want something different. There are more and more of us who can envision a future where sex and pleasure are truly free, where sexuality is more than a packagable commodity or a vector for violence, where women and queer people do not have to choose between desiring sex and desiring our own subjugation. For now, that future is the stuff of heady fantasy – but fantasy, at least, is still free.

4

Cybersexism

Information wants nothing. People want to be free.
Cory Doctorow

There are no girls on the Internet.
4chan

'This is for everyone.' The Internet is a godless place, but that's as close to an in-the-beginning-was-the-word as it gets. The phrase was coined by Tim Berners-Lee, the inventor of the World Wide Web, in time for the London Olympics Opening ceremony, but the principle that the Internet should be socially, economically and politically free, and that anyone anywhere should be able to use it to build new interactive platforms, extend the frontiers of human knowledge or just surf dating forums for cute redheads is basically sound. This is for everyone. Or at least, it was supposed to be.

There was a time, not so long ago, when nerds, theorists and hackers, the first real colonisers of cyberspace, believed that the Internet would liberate us from gender. Science-fiction writers imagined a near future just on the edge of imagination where people's physical bodies would become immaterial as we travelled beyond space and distance and made friends and connections and business deals all over the planet in the space of a split second. Why would it matter, in this brave new networked world, what sort of body you had? And if your body didn't matter, why would it matter if you were a man or a woman, a boy or a girl, or something else entirely?

1998. I'm twelve years old and I've started hanging out in the type of chat forums where everyone will pretend to believe you're a forty-five-year-old history teacher called George. At the same time, the other half of the Internet seems intent on pretending that they are thirteen-year-old schoolgirls from the south coast of England. Amid growing moral panic about paedophiles and teen sluts preying on one another in the murky, unpoliced backwaters of MySpace, I feel something a little akin to freedom. Here, my body, with all of its weight and anxiety, its blood and grease and embarrassing eruptions, is not important; only my words are important. I don't want to be just a girl, because I already knew from experience that girls weren't understood. I want to be what web theorist Donna Haraway calls a cyborg: 'A cyborg is a cybernetic organism, a hybrid of machine and organism, a creature of social reality as well as a creature of fiction. By the late twentieth century, our time, a mythic time, we are all chimeras, theorised and fabricated hybrids of machine and organism . . . I'd rather be a cyborg than a goddess.'[1]

At the turn of the twenty-first century my tits were coming in and I wasn't at all impressed with the messy biopolitics of approaching adolescence. The Internet became part of my life early enough to be the coolest thing ever and late enough that I have memories of Geocities before it became a howling desert rolling with tumbleweed and pixels that don't have the decency to decay, and it seemed like a place where all of the bullshit, the boys and dress codes and harassment and the way grown-up guys were starting to look at me, didn't matter. It was a place where I could be my 'real' self, rather than the self imposed upon me by the ravening maw of girl-world that wanted to swallow me up. It turned out, though, as more and more of our daily lives migrated online, that it did matter if you were a boy or a girl on the Internet. It mattered a very great deal.

Users of the sprawling 4chan forum – a vast, anarchic, nameless playground of the id inhabited mainly but not exclusively by angry young men, which spawned the Anonymous activist network as well as half the stupid cat memes you used to giggle at at work – declared early on that there were 'no girls on the Internet'. That idea sounded like sweet freedom for a lot of us, but it turned out to be a threat.

'In ye olden tymes of 1987, the rhetoric was that we would change genders they way we change underwear,' says Clay Shirky, media theorist and author of *Here Comes Everybody*, '[but] a lot of it assumed that everyone would be happy passing as people like me – white, straight, male, middle class and at least culturally Christian.'[2] Shirky calls this 'the gender closet' – 'people like me saying to people like you, "you can be treated just like a regular normal person and not like a woman at all, as long as we don't know you're a woman.'"[3]

It turned out that the Internet wasn't for everyone. Not really. Not yet. It was for boys, and if you weren't one, you had to pretend to be, or you'd be dismissed. 'I'm fine with people deciding individually that they don't want to identify as female on the Internet – in the same way I'm fine with people deciding not to wear a short skirt if they feel afraid or uncomfortable – but no one should tell you to do that, and imply that if you don't comply you are somehow the one at fault,' says journalist Helen Lewis, who was among the first to speak out against online misogyny in the mainstream press.[4] She says that such advice translates to 'duck, so that the shits abuse someone else'.

I'm seventeen and I'm not allowed on the Internet and it feels like being gagged and blindfolded. During the nine months I spent in a women's ward for the mentally interesting, the Internet was deemed a bad influence, possibly the worst influence, on young girls trying to become healthy, well-behaved women: all that porn, all that trash, all those poisonous pictures of very thin models shared on 'pro-ana' sites where we had encouraged each other to starve down to ecstatic skeletons before we were hospitalised.

The Internet was bad for us. It could only ever be bad for us. So were books and magazines, although television and clothing catalogues were allowed. We needed to be 'contained'. That was the word they used: 'contained'. This was precisely the sort of thinking that I'd tried to get away from by getting sick in the first place, but I wanted to be given a clean certificate of health so I could get out of that terrible place and get on with my life. And so I did what girls have always done in desperate situations, in order to survive when the body is contained. I wrote.

I began to write compulsively in paper notebooks, because computers and smartphones were forbidden. I wrote late into the night and just for myself in a messy, spidery hand that I never showed to anyone, because it was purely mine. Years later when I saw *Girl, Interrupted*, the film of Susanna Kaysen's account of being treated in a women's mental hospital in the 1960s, I was startled that the protagonist does the same, writing frantically in longhand like the pen was a shovel digging her out of the shallow grave of social mores where she'd been buried alive. I wonder if this is why many women write, because it allows us to breathe.

Writing was always freedom for me. I'm aware that that's the sort of observation that belongs in my personal journal, which is why I kept them. By the time I was certified sane enough to walk the streets I had filled twenty volumes, and I continued to do so in the mad years that followed, years of homeless, precarious teenage dicking about and hanging on to a college place with my fingernails while I wrote, learned to be human, wrote, learned to take care of myself, and wrote. And then, sometime after my nineteenth birthday, I discovered LiveJournal, and everything changed.

It was my housemate, who I'd met in a cabaret audition, who turned me on to it. Specifically, she told me that this vast website full of teenage fan fiction, nerdy sub-groups and threaded comments of excitable strangers discussing politics and philosophy and the best place to get coffee in cities we'd never even heard of was where she spent most of her time, and that if I ever wanted to talk to her, despite her being in the next room, I was going to have to join, and post. And so I picked a username out of a hat, this being the year before Facebook, when one's online handle was still a pseudonymous statement of identity, and started writing little blog entries. And that's how I learned to write in public, in a way far more immediate, far more enticing and personal, than the blank, limited audience of the college newspaper could ever be.

I wrote to survive, but I learned how to be a writer online, and so did millions of other women all over the world. And not just how to write, but how to speak and listen, how to understand my own experience and raise my voice. I educated myself online. Grew up online. And on blogs and journals and, later, in the pages of digital magazines, I discovered that I wasn't the only pissed-off girl out there. The Internet made misogyny routine and sexual bullying easy, but first it did something else. It gave women, girls and queer people space to speak to each other without limits, across borders, sharing stories and changing our reality.

The fact that so many women were spending so much time talking to one another online without oversight or policing was part of what led to the feminist revival of the mid-2000s. Suddenly, those of us who had nursed our rage in private realised that we were not alone: there were many thousands of others, all over the world, who felt that there was work still to be done. Young women. Women of colour. Older women. Weird women. Queer women. Mothers. Transgender people of every denomination. To be in such a lightly policed space, to be able to make connections, voice opinions and acquire information without fear of punishment continues empowering when mainstream culture still punishes women who speak up except explicitly to claim victimhood.This is the story of how the net became a universe of infinite possibilities which women are often excluded from building or influencing. You can open your browser and stare into an exhilarating terrain of information exchange and creativity and silly film clips in which women and girls still know, as we know offline, that to participate fully is to risk violence and sexual harassment. The Internet is not monolithic. There are many Internets, and some of them have facilitated new conversations and communities dedicated to raising awareness of women's liberation, gender issues, and there is still so much more to do. But we have a brave new world that looks far too much like the cruel old world. It doesn't have to be that way. Women, girls and everyone who believes that the future of human society should include women and girls as active agents are conspiring to reclaim the Internet for all of us.

CEILING PATRIARCHY IS WATCHING YOU OPERATE

The biggest thing we now learn about sex from the Internet is this: it happens in front of a camera. Welcome to the world of your tits on screen the next day. At nineteen years old, I was one of the first users of Facebook in its first few weeks of viral expansion in Europe, and that means I was among the first cohort to experience the cultural phenomenon of frantic next-day detagging. The lesson you learn, the lesson you have to learn, is that you are always potentially being watched and you must adjust your behaviour accordingly.

Nineteen and getting my picture taken. A warm October night in the front room of a student house where we still hadn't understood the potential pitfalls of prancing around in our pants girls-gone-wild style, snogging and fumbling and demanding pictures to prove it, like any kids excited by mutual attention: look at us kissing. Look at us touching. Pictures or it didn't happen. The next day I find myself tagged on my new profile kissing a female friend, pressed underneath her, hair and sweat and sideboob, giggling at something just off-camera. I detag, but for some reason I leave it up, mistaking the profile archive for the online equivalent of a personal photo album, as so many of us did in the early days. That was before we understood that giving anyone a picture of your breasts, whether a lover or a listed corporation, gives them power over you; before we learned that we had to take care and cover up in cyberspace just like we do in meatspace, in the nominally 'real' world.

Four years later, I'm in a conference hall with sensible shoes and a glass of juice, chatting nervously to an editor who has just given me a job as a political blogger, the magazine's youngest by far. I have won prizes and irritated politicians; suddenly everyone wants to talk to me. Including a bored-looking man in an overstuffed Marks and Spencer's suit, one of the jaundiced breed of lifelong political wonks who begin to look middle-aged at around twenty-two and spend the next thirty years gradually expanding on a diet of other people's principles. He asks if he can speak to me alone.

The wonk tells me that a gossip site has pictures of me, and unless I'm nice to him, unless I 'handle the situation', he's going to use them. Pictures of me at college with my boobs out, kissing another girl – shock, horror, same-sex snogging! Do I remember the picture? I do now. Yes. Well, I'd better watch out, because there are a lot of people who think I ought to be taken down a peg.

The man who sent this message is the sort of scum that rises to the surface of the cybersphere out of our deep and roiling instincts to hurt and shame other people, those who believe that the only true democracy is the democracy of hating. He is the blogger the government fears, the one with dirt on everyone, the one who hates liberals and anyone who dares to have principles in public almost but not quite as much as he hates women.

Particularly young women, or pretty women. Half the traffic to his site is driven by revealing or demeaning pictures of female journalists, politicians and public figures, close-ups on breasts and bottoms, fuelling comment threads full of one-handed rape fantasies where any and every woman in a position of influence can be 'taken down a peg'. He says he's going to put my breasts on the Internet.

He wants me to know he has power over me.

In the few years I have spent as a young woman with a sizeable online following, I have learned just what a fearful thing it still is to be female in public life, how much resilience and stamina it takes to weather the inevitable attacks. One of the most common insults flung at women who speak or write in public is 'attention seeking' – a classic way of silencing us, particularly if we are political.

The fact that 'attention seeking' is still considered a slur says much about the role of women in public life, on every scale. From the moment we can speak, young women are ordered not to do so. Little girls who talk too much, who demand the respect they have earned, are 'attention seeking', and that's very bad. Little boys who do the same are 'confident' or 'engaging'. Men in public life, whether they are celebrities or politicians, rock stars or radio DJs, actors, activists or academics, are almost never accused of being 'attention seeking', with the possible exception of Bono. For a man to seek attention is no crime: attention is men's due. Women, however, are supposed to be silent. We are not accorded the same right to speak. We are still little girls demanding 'attention', and we should learn our place.

The notion that women should be seen and not heard is not confined to the Internet. The popular dead-tree press has always profited from objectifying some women and judging others. Readers are invited to pass judgement upon women's beauty, upon their sexual behaviour, their fitness or unfitness as mothers, the shape of their bodies, the wobbliness of their thighs and their ability to snap back into a size six swimsuit two days after giving birth, and that judgement is the reader's reward for skimming lazily over whatever propaganda the red-tops are peddling that day in the guise of news.

Even as women continue to be under-represented as journalists and editors, body-shaming, objectification and witless woman-hating filler copy remain the stock in trade of the 'professional' media. That trend is only becoming more pronounced as the Internet undercuts its bottom line. Tabloids are now relying more and more on lazy sexism to sell papers, and the news economy of misogyny is more pernicious than ever as it is experienced in real time online.

The woman-hatred of the popular press is in no way separable from the sexism of amateur blogs and web forums: plenty of sexist trolls have regular gigs as print columnists, and the commentariat still behaves like a frat club. Meanwhile, tabloid misogyny such as the *Daily Mail*'s 'sidebar of shame', with its crowing over muffin tops and upskirt shots as bad as anything you'll find on Reddit, legitimises the danker, more covert troughs of gynophobia online.

It is in this climate, in this news economy of misogyny, this society where the male gaze is monetised as never before, that the worst thing any woman or girl can be is 'attention seeking'. Women are supposed to be looked at, but never listened to. We should be seen, but not heard – and God forbid we actually try to direct that attention or appear to enjoy it. If we raise our voices, we are 'attention seeking', and a woman who wants attention, never mind respect, cannot be tolerated. If you're a woman and somebody calls you 'attention seeking', that's a sure way to tell you've made an impact. It's yet another slur that should be a source of pride.

PATRIARCHAL SURVEILLANCE

We cannot perfectly control our online selves any more than we can control the contours of our flesh. Bodies, like data, are leaky. Out of the mess of bodies and blood and bones and pixels and dreams and books and hopes we create this mess of reality we call a self, we make it and remake it. But obtaining a naked or next-to-naked picture of another person gives you power over them.

In this age of images, the right to request no photos is a

sign of truly intimidating social status, of money, power or both, and women, especially young women, almost never have that right. We don't have it in the privacy of our own homes, among friends, in our beds, with our lovers. Especially not with our lovers. In the retail corridor at the New Jersey Porn Expo, shoved in between stall after stall of tacky sex merchandise, was one unobtrusive stand selling hidden cameras, 'for personal security'.

The stallholder was cagey about why there was such a market for concealable recording gear of the type that could be easily stashed out of sight in, say, a bedroom. Some of our customers are just extremely keen on security, he insisted. Watch out for that blinking light, the panopticon eye flashing at the edge of sight.

The surrender of that power can be hugely sensual when it is done with consent – or sickening when it's coerced. Not so long ago, teenage boys would demand joyless fingering or badger female schoolmates into giving them a feel of their developing breasts in order to prove themselves cool and grown-up: nowadays a titty-picture does the job twice as well. A naked picture is never an empty boast: it is proof, proof of your power over another person, and culture still tells us that power over another person is what makes a boy into a man.

Sexist trolls, stalkers, mouth-breathing bedroom misogynists: all of them attack women out of a hatred, in part, for the presence of women and girls in public space, which is what cyberspace remains, for now. Those threats, however, are made infinitely more effective by public officials warning parents of young girls to keep their daughter offline if they don't want them harassed, groomed or 'sexualised', a term that seems to refer to the magical process whereby preteen girls catch a glimpse of some airbrushed boobs on a pop-up ad and are transformed into wanton cybersluts, never to be reclaimed for Jesus.

The message is remarkably similar, in fact, to the lectures one imagines young girls receiving before contraception, legal abortion and the relative relaxation of religious propriety: your sins will never be forgiven. One slip is enough to disgrace you for life. Naked on the Internet is different from being naked anywhere else, because there's always a record: or there could be. We grow up understanding that past indiscretions can never be erased. Don't let your guard down or your skirt up for an instant, or you'll be ruined: not just pictures, but words, promises, furtive late-night search histories will follow you for ever, and you will always be ashamed.

Although the technology is new, the language of shame and sin around women's use of the Internet is very, very old. The answer seems to be the same as it always has been whenever there's a moral panic about women in public space: just stay away. Don't go into those new, exciting worlds: wait for the men to get there first and make it safe for you, and if that doesn't happen, stay home and read a book.

People learn to code by playing in coded space. We learn the Internet by being there, by growing there, by trial and error and risk-taking. If the future is digital, if tech skills and an easy facility with the Internet are to be as essential as they appear for building any kind of career in the twenty-first century, then what are we really saying when we tell girls and their parents that cyberspace is a dangerous place for them to be? We're saying precisely what we've said to young women for centuries: we'd love to have you here in the adult world of power and adventure, but you might get raped or harassed, so you'd better just sit back down and shut up and fix your face up pretty.

Perhaps one reason that women writers have, so far, the calmest and most comprehensive understanding of what surveillance technology really does to the human condition is that women grow up being watched. We grow up learning that someone is always looking at us and checking for misbehaviour, checking that our skirts are long enough, our thighs tight enough, our grades good enough, our voices soft enough. Whether or not anyone is actually watching and checking at any particular moment is less important than the fact that they might be, and if a lapse is observed the penalties will be dire.

Patriarchal surveillance was a daily feature of the lives of women and girls for centuries before the computer in every workplace and the camera in every pocket made it that much easier. The emotional logic of state and corporate surveillance works in very much the same way: the police, our employers, even our parents with network connections may be watching only one in a thousand of our tweets, one in ten thousand of our indiscreet Facebook messages, they may only be watching one in a hundred CCTV cameras of the tens of thousands deployed around every major city, but we must always act as if we are observed and curb our behaviour accordingly.

The Internet is only 'public space', of course, in the way

that a bar, a sidewalk or a shopping-mall are public space: ultimately, someone rich and mysterious owns that space and can kick you out if they don't like what you're doing there. Being aware of surveillance changes how you behave, how you live and love and tie your shoes and eat breakfast, what you say in public, what you read on the subway.

The first people to notice this were men and boys who had not grown up with the expectation of constantly being watched, who were horrified by the proliferation of spyware, private and state surveillance technology, data collection, CCTV cameras on every street corner, long-range police cameras making it impossible to hold a placard in the street without your face ending up on a database. In much of North America, it is now illegal to go out with a mask or bandana over your face. But this is nothing new – at least, not for women. As the journalist Madeline Ashby writes, 'Apparently, it took the preponderance of closed-circuit television cameras for some men to feel the intensity of the gaze that women have almost always been under . . . It took Facebook. It took geo-location. That spirit of performativity you have about your citizenship now? That sense that someone's peering over your shoulder, watching everything you do and say and think and choose? That feeling of being observed? It's not a new facet of life in the twenty-first century. It's what it feels like for a girl.'[5]

Pictures of girls are one of the Internet's major commodities. Melissa Gira Grant, writing in *Dissent* magazine, identifies the activity of self-branding, self-promotion and social work online as a new 'second shift' of women's unpaid work,[6] but it's more than that. It is, in many cases, part of the work you do for your boss, making your company look good, presenting the right image; we're encouraged to imagine that those who pay us, employ us or live with us might be monitoring us at all times, watching what we do and say. Make sure your Twitter feed doesn't embarrass your boss. Make sure your mum doesn't see pictures of what you did last night. Whether or not they actually are watching doesn't matter – we'd better behave, just in case. It takes to another level the traditional pose of paranoia and anal self-retention that has for centuries been called 'femininity'.

One of the most popular terms for all of this is 'NSFW', or 'not safe for work', an abbreviation coined on chat forums to prevent people accidentally opening links to pictures of fannies or gaping sphincters if there's a chance their boss might be peering over their shoulder. Now, however, 'not safe for work' has become shorthand for anything a bit risqué. It's rather appropriate, really, since if two decades of faux-feminist 'empowerment' culture have had a project, it has been to make women 'safe for work', rather than making work safe for women.

Women's sexual bodies are not deemed 'safe for work', either literally or figuratively. We get to choose, online and offline, between the embattled paranoia of a 'good woman', respectful to her seniors and to men, never openly sexual, never asking questions or talking honestly about our own experiences, or the dark, tawdry world of 'bad women', where sluts who dare to have sex are humiliated and hurt. The ultimate power that men feel they hold over women is to drag them from one category to the other, and the Internet, with its boundless recording and publishing capabilities, can make this infinitely easier.

At the same time as girls everywhere are warned to stay offline if we want to preserve a paleo-Victorian notion of our 'reputation', we are told that sex and violence on the Internet isn't 'real'. A robot that can reach through the screen and grab your pink bits has not yet become a standard add-on with every laptop, so sex online can't be real. Can never be coercive.

It might help if we understood, as those who have grown up with half their life on screen instinctively understand, that sex on the Internet is real sex, real pleasure, real passion, whether or not it's 'authentic'. In a world of soft-lighting, speed-dating, pleasure tools that pulse and buzz and tickle and shove and whine in half a million varieties of plastic and rubber and steel, in a world of breast implants, dick implants, of genitals shaved and sliced into pleasing slits and bodies pumped and oiled and choreographed to ram into one another until one of them capitulates, we should have some pillow talk over precisely what we mean by 'real sex'.

What's it like to date, fuck and fall in love when half your social interactions are online? A rash of textbooks and self-help manuals written in a rush of moral panic by contemporary pop psychologists would suggest that it is uniformly abject and exploitative, particularly for young women. Books with titles like *Where Has My Little Girl Gone?* and *Protecting Your Children Online*[7] advise us to keep kids away from the net for as long as possible, instruct parents to implement filtering and censorship systems so that we don't poison young minds or corrupt the innocence of young ladies.

It may seem odd that in a chapter on gender politics on the Internet I've not yet mentioned pornography, which we're repeatedly told is the root of all sexism. I don't buy it. In online porn, as it is everywhere, sex isn't the problem; sexism is the problem. Online misogyny, like any other misogyny, is about power, resentment and frustration, and not about sexual overstimulation, although it can be sexually expressed. Blaming the vicious woman-hatred of men using the Internet to attack women and girls on pornography is, to a very great extent, letting the perpetrators off the hook.

Social media long since overtook porn consumption as the thing most of us use the Internet for most frequently, and social media, because most of it is run by large, terrifying companies with large, terrifying legal teams, is terrified not just of pornography but of sexuality in general. Considering the imperial fuckton of porn available on the Internet, the surprising thing isn't how much it crosses over into our everyday lives, but how much it doesn't. Online and IRL, sex and gender still inhabit two separate worlds. One is a sanitised, sterilised, buttoned-down world of 'professional' conduct where we edit our extracurricular activities for the benefit of our employers and panic over our children being exposed to an accidentally flashed nipple. The other is a rabbit-hole of hardcore heterosexual fucking that relies on its guilty, semi-legal status to disguise the fact that a depressing amount of its content is boring at best and violently misogynist at worst. It's a curious, schizophrenic splitting of sexuality from surface in culture that is supposed to be all surface. Sex, as ever, isn't the problem. People's inability to deal with sex in a way that is not violent, guilty and contemptuous of women and girls is the problem.

For as long as there has been pornography on the web, there have been calls to give state censors the power to shut it down. Blanket censorship of pornography, particularly 'for the sake of the children', would be a poor answer to the sexual dysfunction of our society even if it were possible. For a start, pornography, along with info-piracy and terrorism, has long been used to justify restricting access to the network as a whole, giving governments the power to control what can be seen by whom. It's not about protecting women. It's about controlling people, and so is the crackdown on women's freedom online.

In 2013, British Prime Minister David Cameron initiated a mandatory filtering system for ISPs, obliging every household to 'opt out' of 'violent pornography' and child pornography, and banning certain search terms. It quickly emerged, however, that the filtration system would also block 'violent material', 'extremist' content, 'terrorist-related' content, 'web forums', 'esoteric material' and, of course, 'web-blocking circumvention tools' – a checklist so broad that it would give the state, in cooperation with ISPs, the power to block almost any website.

Note that while using the 'protecting women from harm' line to promote the type of porn-block designed to appeal to swing voters, the same coalition government was kicking single mothers off welfare and stripping funding from domestic violence shelters all over the country.[8] A great deal of harm is done in the name of saving people from themselves, and there is a very real risk that feminist rhetoric will be coopted by people who have no real care for women to push an anti-sex, anti-transparency agenda.

It is terrifically difficult to achieve radical ends by conservative means, and censorship is invariably conservative. Personally, I'm always suspicious of any project that seeks to restrict women's freedom in order to 'protect' us, just as I'm suspicious of any project that seeks to prevent children from finding things out before adults decide they're meant to. Censorship of the Internet is surely not the answer, because the Internet is not the reason for the supposed tide of filth and commercial sexuality we're drowning in; in fact, as I mentioned earlier, young people today have less sex than their parents' generation did at the same age.

One has to ask when, precisely, was the period of human history when the spectrum of sexual adventure from marriage to mud-wrestling was not in some way mercenary, in some way manipulative; if there has ever truly been a time when people got into bed with one another without preconceptions or agendas, when abuse and violence did not take place, when women were not brutalised, when children were not taken advantage of. These things did not begin with the Internet, and the Internet, if anything, is helping us to understand and talk about them over networks of intimacy and anger that did not exist twenty years ago.

I want to come right out and fly the flag for sex, for fucking and for love online. I am a digital romantic. Because sex online is real sex and love online is real love and everything in between is real, too, as real as your hand down your pants, your heart in your mouth. I say this for all of us who've ever felt our breath quicken when a particular userpic pops up on screen. For everyone who marvels that you can use a keyboard to construct a perfect rose that will never have the decency to decay. For the kids sexting each other on sticky smartphones while their parents sleep. For the fan fiction writers sending their horny fairy tales out into the dark like perfumed letters. For the student staying up late to hump a camera for her girlfriend in another timezone. For the Craigslist missed connections and the Chatroulette strangers. For the transsexual teenagers whispering lust and learning in chat rooms while small-town bigots drive drunk through their disappearing fiefdoms. For the World of Warcraft lovers.

Sexuality online is real sexuality, and it's about far, far more than porn. It's the children who meet each other on self-harm forums whispering their most painful everyday secrets until the night when one of them posts in crisis and the others call from across the world in voices so familiar they forget they've never heard each other speak before. It's OKCupid and Fetlife. It's the camgirls and the cryptic personals and the amateur pornographers. It's passive-aggressive status updates, untagging and defriending and broken-hearted blogging. It's the second-dates who tease each other with hyperlinks and the couples who send each other cat-gifs at work. It's every neck-down naked picture I've ever sent to a boy I wanted to screw.

It's the hours positioning yourself on the sheets for the blink of a camera and touching yourself gently when the laptop shuts. It's the shy intellectuals spinning out message-board chats into something seductive, it's all of us who understand that how you fuck can be less important than how you talk about fucking. It's the lonely bedroom blogger flirting with a spambot. It's the bots who want to be loved and the lovers who want to be robots. It's the perverts, the dreamers and the shy, reaching out across the ether and running chilly fingers over each other's forebrains, and it's complicated. It's always complicated. But that doesn't mean it's not human.

SOMEONE IS WRONG ON THE INTERNET

'There's nothing wrong with [her] a couple of hours of cunt kicking, garrotting and burying in a shallow grave wouldn't sort out.'

Like many women with any sort of profile online, I'm used to messages of this sort – the violent rape and torture fantasies, the threats to my family and personal safety, the graphic emails with my face crudely pasted on to pictures of pornographic models performing sphincter-stretchingly implausible feats of physical endurance. This one appeared on a perfectly normal weekday on a racist, misogynist hate-site based in the UK, dedicated to trashing and threatening public figures, mostly women. 'The misogyny here is truly gobsmacking [and] more than a few steps into sadism,' wrote Mary Beard, a television historian who was also hounded by users of the site, Don't Start Me Off. 'It would be quite enough to put many women off appearing in public, contributing to political debate, especially as all of this comes up on Google.'[9]

That, of course, is the point. It doesn't matter if we're young or old, classically attractive or proudly ungroomed, writers or politicians or comedians or bloggers or simply women daring to voice our opinions on Twitter. Any woman active online runs the risk of attracting these kinds of frantic hate-jerkers, or worse. I'm not the only person who has had stalkers hunting for her address, and not so long ago I needed a security detail after several anonymous trolls threatened to turn up to a public lecture I was giving. I could go on.

It'd be nice to think that the rot of rank sexism was confined to fringe sites. The truly frightening thing, though, is that the people sending these messages are often perfectly ordinary men holding down perfectly ordinary jobs: the person who wrote the drooling little note to me above and ran the site it appeared on was an estate agent called Richard White, who lived in Sidcup, outer London, with a wife and kids, and just happened to run a hate website directed at women and minorities.[10] The Internet recreates offline prejudices and changes them, twists them, makes them voyeuristic, and anonymity and physical distance makes it easier for some individuals to treat other people as less than human.

But it's not just individuals having horny fun trolling anyone who seems like they might react. It's not even just those outside the so-called 'professional' sphere of online commentary and debate. In recent years, violent misogyny in comment threads and blogs has become an everyday feature of political conversation on the web. Here are just some of the things that have been written about me personally in the past few months in the comments section of the website Order Order, a blog followed by politicians and journalists across the country, whose editors are considered part of mainstream political debate in the UK. These are a selection from the comments that the editors did not deem worthy of deletion at the time:

> Perhaps Sharia might be a good thing after all, if Ms Penny was not allowed out without a member of her Family and we did not have to look at her face, also we could stone her to death, my favourite though would be a Public Hanging or Decapitation, all judging by her views, to be acceptable behaviour. Perhaps she should be Circumcised, only sew up her mouth.

> Call me old fashioned bt this young lady shouid [sic] be whipped through the streets of London before being made to suck Ken Livingstones cock as people throw shit at the pair of them.[11]

The person who wrote the latter is clearly a seventeenth-century burgher, which makes you wonder what he's doing in the onanistic comment threads of British political wonk-sites, and it'd be funny if there weren't hundreds more just like him.

It's important to stress that I'm no outlier in having this experience – although I did work as a political journalist in Britain at a time when certain women and girls were singled out to be made examples of by the angry old men in cardigans running most of the dead-tree media. It's not every woman who writes online or runs a blog or plays video-games, but it's many of us, and it could be any of us. And threats to hurt and rape and kill are not always less distressing when they don't come with an explicit expectation of follow-through in physical reality.

These messages are intended specifically to shame and frighten women out of engaging online, in this new and increasingly important public sphere. If we respond at all, we're crazy, hysterical overreacting bitches, censors, no better than Nazis, probably just desperate for a 'real man' to fuck us, a 'real man' like the men who lurk in comment threads threatening to rip our heads off and masturbate into the stumps.

The idea that this sort of hate speech is at all normal needs to end now. The Internet is public space, real space; it's increasingly where we interact socially, do our work, organise our lives and engage with politics, and violence online is real violence. The hatred of women in public spaces online is reaching epidemic levels and it's time to end the pretence that it's acceptable and inevitable.

The most common reaction, the one those of us who experience this type of abuse get most frequently, is: suck it up. Grow a thick skin. 'Don't feed the trolls' – as if feeding them were the problem. The *Telegraph*'s Cristina Odone wrote that 'Women in public arenas get a lot of flak – they always have. A woman who sticks her head above the parapet is asking for brickbats.'[12]

Asking for it. By daring to be visibly female in public life, we're asking to be abused and harassed and frightened, and so is any person with the temerity to express herself while in possession of a pair of tits.

It's an attitude so quotidian that only when you pause to

pick it apart does its true horror become apparent. I am contacted, not every day, but most weeks, by young women who want to build lives as journalists or activists but are afraid of the possible backlash. Every time I receive one of these letters, I get a lurch of guilt: should I tell them the truth? Should I tell them that sometimes I've been so racked with anxiety by the actions of trolls and stalkers that I've been afraid to leave the house, that I've had to call in the police, that there's every chance they might too? Or should I tell them to be brave, to take it on the chin, to not be frightened, because their fear, their reticence to speak, is precisely what the trolls want to see most of all?

I always hesitate over whether or not to speak about this. For one thing, I don't want to let on just how much this gets to me. Nobody does. It's what the bullies want, after all. They want evidence that you're hurting so they can feel big and hard, like Richard White in his ridiculous Twitter profile picture, which shows him with beefy arms aggressively folded and his face obscured by a cross. Nobody wants to appear weak, or frightened, or make out that they can't 'take it' – after all, so few people complain. Maybe we really are just crazy bitches overreacting?

And so we stay silent as misogyny becomes normalised. We're told to shut up and accept that abuse of this vicious and targeted kind just happens and we'd better get used to it. While hatred and fear of women in traditionally male spaces, whether that be the Internet or the Houses of Parliament, is nothing new, the specific, sadistic nature of online sexist and sexual harassment is unique, and uniquely accepted – and it can change.

Not all online sexism is intended to hurt women. Some of it is intended to impress other men, with hurting women as a regrettable but necessary side-effect. A great deal of misogyny has always been a matter between men, performed by men and boys to impress those they consider peers, and forums, games and blogs are no different.

When men say that casual online sexism, as separate from the personal femicidal misogyny that many women receive when they venture into online spaces men think are theirs alone, is 'just banter', they really mean it.

Germaine Greer once wrote that women had no idea how much men hate them.[13] Well, now we do. The Internet has a way of making hidden things visible, of collapsing contexts so that the type of banter that might once have been appropriate at a frat party exists on the same Twitter feeds where fifteen-year-olds are starting feminist campaigns. Combine that with the disinhibition provided by time-delay and anonymity and you have a recipe for the sort of gynophobic, racist and homophobic rage that women and men who are its targets often find incredibly frightening.

Parts of the Internet still behave like men-only spaces, even though they almost never are. Misogyny, as well as racism and homophobia, is played as a shibboleth, a way of marking out territory, not necessarily to keep women away, but to scare off anyone considered too easily offended, which in practice rarely includes men. It's a joke, certainly, the kind of weak, cruel joke whose humour revolves around exclusion, the kind of joke one is meant to 'take' (can't you take a joke?) in the way one takes a punch. It's the way men have always spoken about women in private, and the reason it looks new is that women have never had so much instant and intimate access to those spaces before, where we could observe men speaking about us as they have for centuries when they thought we weren't watching. The power to watch men back is something the web affords women, but men haven't quite realised that yet.

Right now, the beginning of a backlash against online misogyny is under way. Women and girls and their allies are coming together to expose gender violence online and combat structural sexism and racism offline, collecting stories on hashtags like the #Everydaysexism and #Aufshcrei and #Solidarityisforwhitewomen. Projects like this turn sexism and racism from something you have to sit and experience alone into something that can be turned back on your attackers, forcing men who really aren't as ignorant as they'd like to be to understand women's experience in a new way, to understand that the stories they grew up hearing about how the world worked might not be the only stories out there. When bigotry is forced to see itself through the eyes of another, the reaction can be grotesque.

In 2012, the blogger Anita Sarkeesian launched a crowd-funding project to create a short film series, *Tropes vs. Women*,[14] which set out to explain the basic, lazy sexist plotlines of many videogames. The self-satisfied geeksphere exploded with rage; one user even created a flashgame called Beat Up Anita Sarkeesian, where users could click on her face and make blood, cuts and bruises appear. Sarkeesian faced down her abusers and made the series anyway. It was a hit.

Six months later, when feminist campaigner Caroline

Criado-Perez successfully campaigned to get a woman's face featured on British banknotes, she was inundated with rape threats on social media.[15] She shared examples of the messages she received from sexist trolls over five days: 'Everyone jump on the rape train > @CCriadoPerez is conductor' was one; 'This Perez one just needs a good smashing up the arse and she'll be fine' was another. Criado-Perez decided to stand up and fight back, demanding that Twitter take more responsibility for abuse on its platform and starting a global conversation about the normalisation of violent misogyny online. Technically, threats of rape and violence are already criminal, and many social media companies, including Twitter, already have rules against abuse and harassment. Just like in the offline world, however, there is a chasm of difference between what is technically illegal and what is tacitly accepted when it comes to violence against women, and the fight back is less about demanding new laws than ensuring existing ones are taken seriously.

Some people claim that the fight back against cybersexism is itself 'censorship'. Some website owners claim that promoting and publicising sadistic misogyny is merely respecting the 'freedom of speech' of anyone with a lonely hard-on for sick rape fantasies. That sort of whinging isn't just disingenuous, it's terrifically offensive to anyone with any idea of what online censorship actually looks like.

As I write, there is a real fight going on to keep the Internet as free as possible from government interference, a fight to free speech and information from the tyranny of state and corporate control. Without going into it too much here, the Internet is full of people who have spent their lives, risked their lives and even lost their lives in that fight. To claim that there's some sort of equivalence between the coordinated attack on net neutrality and digital freedom going on across the world and the uninterrupted misogyny of comment-thread mouth-breathers doesn't just take the biscuit, it pinches the whole packet and dribbles ugly bile-flecked crumbs into the keyboard.

According to the current logic of online misogyny a woman's right to self-expression is less important by far than a man's right to punish her for that self-expression. What appears to upset many of these people more than anything else is the idea that any woman or girl, anywhere, might have a voice, might be successful, might be more socially powerful than they themselves are – at least, that's the message I get every time I'm told that I've got a lot to say for myself, and my silly little girl's mouth could be more usefully employed sucking one of the enormous penises that these commentators definitely all possess. In 2011 I wrote that a woman's opinion was the mini-skirt of the Internet; if she has one and dares to flaunt it in public, she is deemed to deserve any abuse that comes her way – she was asking for it.[16]

Since then, the situation appears to have deteriorated, not just for women in public life but for women in public full stop. The Internet is a many-to-many medium. It gives readers and audience-members a right to reply to those writers and politicians who, in the pre-digital age, enjoyed the freedom to expostulate and make pronouncements without having to listen to their readers or listeners beyond the odd angry letter in the paper. And that's great. I remain glad that I grew up as a journalist in the age of the Internet;

I am used to writing for an audience that is responsive and engaged, to listening to constructive criticism and acknowledging it where it's appropriate. There's a world of difference, however, between the right to reply and the right to abuse, threaten and silence.

To be human is, in almost every case, to crave two things above all else: intimacy and information. The Internet offers us a superabundance of both, which is one of the reasons it sends existing power structures into a panic. Whether it's women and minorities fighting for the right to be understood as fully human, or citizens fighting for access to information they're not supposed to have, the impulse is always to censor, or to attempt to censor. It is extremely ironic, then, that when misogynist trolls are called out on their behaviour, they claim that it's an attack on their 'freedom of speech'.

The hypocrisy is breathtaking, brain-aching. These people talk without irony of their right to free expression while doing everything in their power to hurt, humiliate and silence any woman with a voice or a platform, screeching abuse at us until we back down or shut up. They speak of censorship but say nothing of the silencing in which they are engaged. I have even been told, with apparent sincerity, that using the 'block' button on Twitter to prevent anybody who has posted threats of violence against me is actually an attack on the troll's freedom of speech – no apparent distinction being made between the right to express your views and the right to have your ugliest half-thoughts paid attention to.

The Internet has pressing, urgent problems with freedom of speech, and none of them have anything to do with men's right to harass and threaten women with impunity. 'Imagine this is not the Internet but a public square,' comments the writer Ally Fogg. 'One woman stands on a soapbox and expresses an idea. She is instantly surrounded by an army of 5,000 angry people yelling the worst kind of abuse at her in an attempt to shut her up. Yes, there's a free speech issue there. But not the one you think.'[17]

Freedom of speech does not include the freedom to abuse and silence others with impunity. It doesn't even include the right to be paid attention to. Imagine that that was 'real life'. Imagine that any woman standing up in parliament, or in a lecture theatre or in a room full of her friends to talk about her own experiences learned to anticipate violence, threats and taunting if she happened to upset the men. Actually, you don't have to imagine, because that still happens every day, even in the nominally liberated West. Everywhere, people in positions of privilege warp and misuse the idea of 'free speech' to shut down and silence everyone else's right to speak freely. Freedom of speech, for so many people used to the comfort of not having to examine their lives, simply means freedom from criticism and responsibility.

In the case of cybersexism, it is deeply offensive to the many, many activists, hackers and developers who have given their time, imperilled their jobs and sometimes risked their lives to keep governments like the United States from clamping down on free Internet usage to describe women speaking about feminism online as a threat to 'freedom of speech'.

The whole point of the Internet is that it allows many voices to speak at once. That's what the network is. The sudden presence of women in great and vocal numbers online doesn't prevent men from using the Internet, because this isn't primary school, and nobody is actually allergic to girls.

AND THE GEEK SHALL INHERIT THE EARTH

This is what I want every nerd boy in my life to understand: we were there too. The other geeks and weird kids whose lives were hellish at school, who escaped into books and computers, who stayed up all night with our faces uplit by humming screens looking for transcendence, dreaming of elsewhere. We were there too, but you didn't see us, because we were girls. And the costs of being the geek were the same for us, right down to the sexual frustration, the yearning, the being laughed at, the loneliness. And then we went online, which was supposed to be where nobody could tell that you were a shy, speccy loser with no friends, only to find ourselves slut-shamed and screamed at if we gave away that we might be female. For us, there was no escape. We had to fight the same battles you did, only harder, because we were women and we also had to fight sexism, some of it from you, and when we went looking for other weird kids to join our gang, we were told we weren't 'real geeks' because we were girls.

Geek misogyny is its own special flavour of bullshit, and it's part of the infrastructure of how gender works online. I'm using the terms 'nerd' and 'geek' interchangeably, in part because a great many people who are both have clear ideas on the distinction between the two, and everyone has different ideas about what that distinction is. In the 1900s, a 'geek' was a member of a travelling circus who bit the heads off live chickens to entertain local yokels. Today it's more likely to be a person who works with computers and gets very excited about comics. What unites the two, and what's important about geeks and nerds, is a sense of being an outsider, a fascination with learning, and specialist knowledge.

That specialist knowledge could be coding, or it could be literature, or it could be where exactly to bite down on a cockerel's spine to make the arterial blood gush most gruesomely over your shirt. Either way, it's probably something your parents don't really understand.

The idea that women can't ever be proper geeks or 'real' nerds is perhaps the most insidious part of the misogynist defence of geek space. It's what leads to terms like 'fake geek girl', to the assumption that women who like science fiction or comics or gaming or technology don't really know what they're talking about. A close friend of mine who works as a senior editor at a major science-fiction publishing house is regularly assumed to be somebody's girlfriend – or a promotional 'booth babe' – at conferences and conventions.

We have to take back the word 'geek', not just women and girls, but anyone out there who is fed up of the assumption that being a geek means sitting in your parents' basement in a failed start-up hoodie, hating women. One of the most upsetting things about the way nerd culture has been incorporated into the mainstream, quite apart from personal childish annoyance when something you've been into for ages becomes cool, is the absorption of many of the radical, egalitarian impulses of traditional nerd culture into a stereotype. It's doubly upsetting when that stereotype has some basis in truth.

The social narrative of the successful geek has become the twenty-first century's Horatio Alger tale of the victorious underdog, the outcast made good, but the one mode for triumph in this story is acquisition – specifically, acquisition of hot chicks and a pile of money.

This is the story of Geek Triumph. It's a short story, and you can find it in every comic shop, DVD aisle and entrepreneurial business memoir. The Geek Boy has an awful time at school. He is lonely. He has no friends, or few friends, and is bullied. Nobody understands his special genius, and the hot, popular girl who is the object of his late-night tissue-box fantasies won't even look his way. Geek Boy, however, has a way to escape this otherwise Dantean nightmare of post-pubescent torment: he is smart. He is really smart. He uses his smartness to make a pile of cash and get the girl, becoming the ultimate neo-capitalist patriarch without even having to change out of his slogan T-shirt.

The getting of the girl is a pivotal part of this story. The story wouldn't work if the girl wasn't got. The hot girl, in fact, is the motivating factor, both the prize and the peril – she is the Dark Crystal, the One Ring, the McGuffin that makes the rest of the narrative hang together. She isn't a real person, of course – that'd be inconvenient. In some variations of this story, the pretty, popular girl gets her comeuppance – usually humiliating rejection by the now universally popular Geek Boy – and is replaced by a less popular but equally pretty girl who has been pining for the protagonist since Act 1. The trouble is that if the story doesn't work out that way, and in an economic system designed so most of us lose it really doesn't usually work that way, people start looking for someone to blame.

'The web is geared towards constructing subcultures and for many years operated as a subculture,' says Maha Rafi Atal, a journalist who writes on gender and tech for Forbes and other sites. 'There is a real truth to the idea that the men – and at the time it was mostly men – who first built the web were at the margins of social power in a traditional, high-school-cafeteria sense – and because a lot of them were young, the symbol of the social belonging they didn't have was their inability to connect with women.'[18] Even though everyone is now online, including the jocks, cheerleaders and cool kids, Atal explains that 'the culture still operates on the basis of woman as the inscrutable enemy'.

The story of the Genius in the Basement is the creation myth of many of our social networks just as the story of the founding fathers is the creation myth of American capitalism: it may only tell part of the story, but it's the part that makes the rest easier for the most privileged to understand. The Oscar-winning 2010 film *The Social Network*, which spins out the fractious formative years of Facebook into a heart-warming tale of one smart loser's triumph over romantic adversity to become the world's youngest billionaire, tells just this story.

In the first scene, a young Mark Zuckerberg, played by Jesse Eisenberg, is dumped by his girlfriend. He takes revenge by using his superior tech skills to create a site that allows his fellow students, presumably men, to rate the attractiveness of women at their college based on pictures grabbed without permission from Harvard servers, blogging sexual slurs about his recent ex at the same time. The site, FaceMash, goes viral: Zuckerberg has created an incredibly clever toy, broken codes, beaten the system, and made a tool that reduces every woman in his peer group to their value as a sexual object. He's the man, and they are just women, and he can control them; he has won. We see Zuckerberg applying the basic principles of this system to construct a social platform on which, ten years later, a quantifiably large proportion of human interaction takes place. Welcome to Facebook.

In the film, men who have been humiliated by women have had the last laugh: they have used their smarts to monetise social capital, to turn every one of us into a digital product constantly engaged in a 'second shift' of self-promotion, curating our online presence, developing our brand, updating our photos to make ourselves look like we're having the best and most employable time possible, all the while making money for Facebook and its spin-off sites. Capitalism, technology and the revenge of the socially excluded have come together to create a world where all of us, particularly women and girls, are products, all social capital shall be categorised for cash, and the Geek shall inherit the earth.

The number of women working in technology isn't just low – it is falling. Only 7 per cent of tertiary degrees in computing are taken by women and girls, and women leave the industry at all levels. Yahoo boss Marissa Mayer estimates that 15 to 17 per cent of Silicon Valley engineers are women, and just 20 per cent of engineering and computer science majors in the United States are female.[19] Mayer, who didn't become a regular Internet user until she was in college,[20] disproves the rule that once we've failed to teach any given generation of girls about computers in elementary school, it's too late for them. Tech skills can be picked up as late as you like, as long as you don't believe that your brain is temperamentally unsuited to the task, as many girls and women do.

Of course, Mayer proved her credentials as a leader in a land built and run by nerd men by taking away Yahoo employees' right to work from home[21] – making the company yet another Silicon Valley leader structured in a way that excludes women who have children, or who want them someday, from full participation. Tech is a notoriously hostile sector for anyone whose lifestyle doesn't happen to chime with that of a single guy working ten-hour days, and it's getting worse.

Kate Losse was one of Facebook's earliest employees, and her 2012 book *The Boy Kings* tells the inside story of the company as it developed.[22] 'I wrote the book because in working there . . . I noticed things that weren't being articulated and that are really important in understanding how social technology is affecting us,' Losse told me over IM. 'One thing I noticed is how driven by women's images and social media labour Facebook and other social technologies are. But that fact isn't well recognised or rewarded by these companies for the most part.

'There was this assumption that a very specific kind of person made tech products and that he was usually a young male entrepreneur with specific tastes and values and that he was somehow this genius of social media.'

This is not, in fact, the way the Internet works, and it's not the way geekdom works, either. Being a geek isn't about getting your revenge on the people who bullied you at school. It's not about hanging out in dark bedrooms hating women. Being a geek is so much more than that. It's about being curious, and clever. Being a geek is about making things, and fixing things, and taking things apart to see how they work, sometimes lines of code and sometimes countries. It's about being excited, tremendously excited about awesome things like stories and games and comics and books and films and not ever having to apologise for thinking those things are brilliant. It's about learning, and creating, and wanting. It's about understanding, on a fundamental level, that being smart is more important than being strong, and who you are and where you come from doesn't matter as long as you've got curiosity and guts.

One of the most important things to understand about cybersexism is that it comes from a place of pain, a place of fear and hurt that translates into violent incomprehension in the most personal ways. It is not, of course, the responsibility of those abused to make their abusers feel better, but compassion is a useful tool for understanding as well as a way forward.

For geekdudes, the Internet is a safe space. It always has been. Sure, it's also a weird warren full of casual violence and bullying, but it's their weird warren of casual violence and bullying, and unlike what those who live there like to call 'real life', they know the rules. They made up some of the rules. They grew up on the Internet, and they pride themselves on knowing its language and customs better than anybody else, whether or not they actually do.

It starts at school, like almost everything else. The sense that being smart and a bit strange makes you a target for violence, means you're not a real man. It seems a cliché to point out that geeks, nerds and boffins of all kinds, anyone who was a bit clever or unorthodox or both and lacked the talent or volition to conceal it, anyone who was bad at sports and flirting, we all had to deal with daily harassment and ostracisation, usually for years. It affects everything. For boys, being tormented by jocks creates an embattled masculinity. That embattled masculinity sometimes finds a home online and a target in women, preferably women who are far away and can't fight back.

One of the most important ways in which boys prove their social value, prove that they are or will shortly become men, is by exerting power over women: sexual power, physical power, the power to bully and threaten and intimidate and control. Sexism is a status play. At school, the fact that geekdudes are normally lower down in the status hierarchy is part of what creates the unique flavour of rage spicing up the murky broth of nerd misogyny, and the rage is knotted up with sexual frustration.

The creation myths of geek misogyny hold that almost every transformative piece of technology in history was invented by a man to impress a woman, who was normally ungrateful. A viral blog post by Cracked.com editor David Wong described 'why no amount of male domination will ever be enough': 'Go look at a city skyline. All those skyscrapers? We built those to impress you[.] All those sports you see on TV? All of those guys learned to play purely because in school, playing sports gets you laid. All the music you hear on the radio? All of those guys learned to sing and play guitar because as a teenager, they figured out that absolutely nothing gets women out of their pants faster. It's the same reason all of the actors got into acting.

'All those wars we fight? Sure, at the upper levels, in the halls of political power, they have some complicated reasons for wanting some piece of land or access to some resource. But on the ground? Well, let me ask you this – historically, when an army takes over a city, what happens to the women there?'[23]

Whoa. Hold it right there. What happens to the women in occupied cities? Exactly the same as what happens to the women when players attack a town in a MMORG game: they get raped and murdered. Wong interprets that, on behalf of the lady-fancying male Internet-using community, as a massive compliment. 'You're all we think about, and that gives you power over us. And we resent you for it,'[24] writes Wong, choosing to elide the experience of the millions of men who do not think about women in that particular way. It hasn't occurred to Wong, and to every other angry man in front of his laptop, that not all 'women' have this power, because the category 'women' does not, in fact, include only 'women David Wong wants to have sex with'.

Moreover, perhaps even the women who do have this kind of power don't actually want it. Perhaps we consider it a raw deal that the power to turn men on is the only sort of power we're allowed, and that we're punished and resented and attacked and bullied and brutalised and killed for having it. Guys, listen up: we're not conspiring with your boners against you. Women are people, not walking bags of pheromones and interestingly arranged body fat, and we like to be treated as such.

In 2003, a list of 'Geek Social Fallacies' – the particular social hang-ups common to many circles of nerds, hackers, gamers and oddballs[25] – went viral online, and ten years later it's still an important reference point for members of the communities that built much of the architecture of the Internet. The first and most important of these is that 'Ostracisers are evil'. Geeks of every gender and background, having experienced the pain of being shunned and excluded, are loath to exclude anyone else, even if their behaviour is offensive, creepy or violent. This can lead, in groups that would otherwise consider themselves progressive, to the tolerance of vicious bigotry. In some circles of professional nerds it's openly admitted that sexism and homophobia have long been tolerated, or written off as 'ironic', as long as the person spreading such hatred is a good coder or a decent gamer. A long history of learned defensiveness leads nerds to come together to protect any member of their group, whatever they've done. It's an understandable impulse – right up to the point where you realise that tolerance of bigotry automatically ostracises everyone who happens to be a woman, or queer, or frightens them away from social and professional groups in which 'white, male, cis and straight' is the default player setting.

To the list of Geek Social Fallacies, one might well add 'the fallacy of persecution'. Slowly but surely, being a geek – particularly a tech geek – has become a position of power. A job at Google or Facebook is for the young people of the twenty-teens what a job in finance was in the 1980s: a whole new world of pseudo-meritocracy, with its own laws and customs that happen to be that much easier to negotiate if you're a white, straight, middle-class cis guy, however much the recruitment drivel claims otherwise.

That doesn't mean that being a geek, a nerd or a weird smart kid at school is any easier now than it was ten years ago, and it certainly hasn't stopped nerds from being mercilessly made fun of in a certain type of bro-comedy that still dominates mainstream Hollywood programming, from *The Big Bang Theory* to *The IT Crowd* to any half-rate thriller where the hilariously sexless scientist helps the jock hero to triumph. But the territory has fundamentally changed, and I don't simply mean that thick glasses have become cool – believe me, I hate that too.

Part of the problem is the suspicion that girls just aren't as clever as boys. It's not been modish to say that out loud for decades, but it is implied every time excuses are made for why women remain vastly under-represented in tech, in politics, in business, in the top rungs of academia. Just look at the evidence: we apparently have equality now, and yet there are still far fewer women in 'smart jobs' than men. We're told unremittingly that feminism has achieved all of its aims, and that even if it hasn't, tech and research are fields of perfect meritocracy, so this must be a process of natural selection. If women aren't making it to the top, that obviously means that they simply aren't good enough, aren't bright enough, aren't committed enough.[26]

In her excellent book *Delusions of Gender*, neuroscientist Cordelia Fine meticulously debunks every cod theory attributing social sex class to hard-wired 'brain differences'. The many available studies that show no practical difference whatsoever in the cognitive, reasoning or structural processing power of 'male' and 'female' brains[27] tend to get far less press coverage and be less high profile than those claiming that the social mores of white, suburban 1950s America were laid down in prehistoric times – despite the fact that they are consistently more sound. Fine quotes many of the world's most respected psychiatrists and neuroscientists, such as Professor Simon Baron-Cohen, peddling such codswallop as: 'The female brain is predominantly hard-wired for empathy. The male brain is predominantly hard-wired for understanding and building systems.'[28]

This, in fact, is the most persistent delusional artefact of what is known as evolutionary psychology. Women are good at feeling and men are good at thinking. Women have more 'social' intelligence, are better able to 'multitask', whereas men are better at things that require the sort of focus that can only be achieved when your wife or girlfriend is sorting out dinner. Women can be almost as smart as men, but we're smarter at different things, things like nurturing, listening, taking care of other people, managing social systems, throwing parties, publicising events and inventions men are in charge of, organising the diaries and offices of men that they might better concentrate on the important work, and, of course, raising children. Men, in other words, are good at doing, making and building things; women are good at making life easier for men. We're not less smart, we're just different smart. Smart at things that don't involve being listened to or making an impact on the world. You know, different smart.

It's a eugenics of gender that would be seen for the throat-closingly vile propaganda it is were the tests being done on people of different races, ethnicities or sexual preferences. And yet these myths persist because they are soothing, comforting, because they provide a halfway rational basis for the prejudices that poison our society.

Otherwise rational individuals cling to bad science to justify the ongoing dismissal of women in exactly the same way people once clung to religion to provide that same justification: once, women didn't go into research and engineering because God had designed them to be full-time mothers; today, women don't go into research and engineering because evolution designed them to be bad at maths and better at babies. This is, apart from anything else, a terrible misuse of a respected theory.

CHANGING THE SCRIPT

I'm twenty-seven and I work and write and hunt down stories online, and right now I'm following the Pirate Party, the online-freedom activist group that became a global political movement, as it seeks to get its first representatives in a national parliament, in Iceland. In a bar where all the candidates, hackers and gamers and nerds to a man and woman, are gathered for drinks and strategy, someone starts talking about feminism, and how it makes the men feel.

I join the conversation. It's a discussion I've had before. It encompasses how the guys feel when their idols are accused of rape, what they think 'patriarchy' means, whether women are really just overreacting – and their fear of being misunderstood. Their fear is legitimate; there is pain on both sides. Then one of them, a hacker called Jason who has been belittling the women at the table, says something that will stay with me for a long time. 'I think you're wrong,' he says, 'but I'm prepared to accept that I might not have all of the information.'

Why does he think women are wrong about how they experience gendered violence?

'I'm not saying that. I just feel you're trying to define me, and trying to define men, and I don't like it.'

Has he considered that he might not have all the information about himself?

Jason manages to convey an expression of sudden quiet enlightenment under a thick and ponderous neck-beard, which is quite a feat. Over the next three days of reporting we continue the discussion. This guy wants to learn. He isn't the first geek guy I've met who has come suddenly to the understanding that their information about how the world works is flawed and incomplete, nor the first to want to change it.

Geeks aren't just the problem. Geeks are also the solution. The Internet may perpetuate prejudice and facilitate gendered violence, but it also helps us fight it. When the story of Todd's suicide hit the press, Anonymous and other amorphous online activist groups got together to expose men who they accused of blackmailing her with nude photos. Shortly afterwards, misogynist trolls like 'Violentacrez' – a man named Michael Brutsch, who was behind Reddit sub-groups like 'jailbait' and 'creepshots' – began to be hunted down and identified by journalists or private individuals.[29] As I write, a new mood of online vigilantism is beginning to take hold of the net, whereby people with a new understanding of misogyny and what it means aren't prepared to wait for society to fix itself. You can hack anything, after all, and that includes sexism.

Vigilantism is what happens when the laws of the land are not fit for purpose. Right now the Internet is outstripping the conventional court system when it comes to digging out information about rapists and other sexual predators. When geeks decide to take up the cause of feminism, they are a fearful thing. The Internet is a new country, without laws or borders, and there is no reason for the old rules of men-talk-women-get-fucked to apply here for very much longer.

A networked society is only as good as the networks upon which it is built. A network that dehumanises women and denies them full, free access to the same channels men enjoy is simply not a network that works properly, and geeks, nerds and everyone who cares about the Internet as a free and open space need to understand that their network is no longer fit for purpose. Our system is broken. It needs to be updated.

As in cyberspace, so in meatspace: the networks in which we love and fuck are the same networks in which we do politics, educate one another, fight the government, change the world. If the Internet is revolutionising politics, keeping girls off the net, or at least keeping us cowed and complicit online, it is a way of shutting us out of that revolution.

The Internet is a political place, if it is a place, and a place where politics is being altered for ever. Young people, disenfranchised people, ordinary workers sitting at home with tired faces uplit by lonely laptop screens are working out new ways of finding one another in this networked world, building platforms and lines of communication that have, over the past half-decade, routinely outpaced and outsmarted governments. Every time an individual state attempts to crack down on freedom of speech online it reassures net denizens that online activism and online organising are powerful.

The Internet is a real place. It's where we live and work and fight and fuck and make friends. Harassment, intimidation and silencing online are more than 'just words', and not just because they are sometimes, in my experience, photos of your head pasted on porn, cartoons of you being beaten up, or phone calls whispering about your sexual history. Whoever cooked up the idiot axiom about sticks and stones breaking bones but words being essentially harmless never knew a teenager bullied to suicide by online taunting.

Once the geek community finally wakes up to the fact that the harassment, bullying and intimidation of women online is a clear threat to the principles of freedom of speech and egalitarianism, the social space of the Internet will start to look very different. Boys grow up believing that they are the hero in their own story; girls have to learn not to see themselves as a supporting character in someone else's saga. Fortunately, the Internet lets you choose your own adventure. Systems can be rewritten. Protocols updated. The social architecture we're building online today will be the one the next generation grows up in, and if that looks too much like the one we did, for all our talk of futurism, we've fucked up. There's time to turn it around. The system adapts, and we can rewrite it so it works better – or we can make it a playroom for the prejudices of the past. It's up to us.

5

Love and Lies

To be the object of desire is to be
defined in the passive case.
Angela Carter, *The Sadeian Woman*

In New York City, romance is a bloodsport. It could hardly be anything else in this place that casts everything from brunch to bunking up as a business opportunity. Nonetheless, when I arrived at the age of twenty-five, I had expected the boggling rigamarole of dinner-dates, calendar synchronisation, expectations, hook-ups and heartbreaks I'd seen on various imported TV series to be somewhat of an exaggeration, if not an outright American lie. But then again, I thought that about breakfast pizza and Bible-belt fundamentalists. Both of those turned out to exist, too.

New York is the holy city of industrial romance. I saw it first on television, the glowing altar to permissible passion that skulks in every single girl's living room. My mother watches *Sex and the City* like the unlapsed Catholics in her family went to Mass. I watch it with her like going to church with Nanna as a child, less out of belief than out of anxiety to share the stories that moved the adults I cared for.

Sex and the City, the long-running, now dated series, starring wealthy professional women living lives of erotic luxury in Manhattan, was supposed to mean freedom – the ultimate freedom we were permitted as women – shoes and shopping and fucking, the aspirational routine of wealthy white indulgence which most of us could only fantasise about. The vibrator plugged in next to a window with a view of the Twin Towers.

And yet somehow, so little had changed. Because despite their money, their privilege, their friendships, the great sex they seemed to be having, the jobs they apparently had, although they rarely seemed to actually do them, the weird spoilt child-women of *Sex and the City* were still miserable, still looking for something – if they hadn't been, there would have been no story. What they were looking for was what every woman and girl is still, always, supposed to be looking for: love. For monogamous, marriage-minded romantic partnership with the man of their dreams. Every girl's story was a love story.

This particular kind of love was what the women of *Sex and the City* and all their millions of fans were meant to want in the liberated 2000s. When they didn't get it, or when they got it but somehow it didn't live up to their expectations, they were bereft, for all that the show was supposed to personify the Strong Woman in her white, wealthy, Western incarnation, all 400-dollar heels and jobs squeezed in around the designated time for weeping into one's cosmopolitan. It demonstrated that even the most powerful, liberated women the world had ever known could still be brought low by love, could still be ruined by disappointment in the quest for love.

New York is the coliseum of competitive dating. The city is lousy with otherwise decent young men who expect to spend their twenties and early thirties devastating women, and with otherwise sensible young women who develop a chilly, shark-eyed aspect as they speak quite seriously of five-year plans and appear to be calculating the number of calories in a human heart.

The whole business is highly ritualised; there is a set schedule for the first kiss, first fuck, first conversation about whether or not you're seeing other people, and whatever you do, you can't say the 'L' word too soon, or risk spooking your prey.

Even being gay doesn't necessarily get you out of it. The fight for marriage equality has been won on a moral and legal level in many states and countries, which is obviously wonderful, in that LGBT people deserve the right to ruin their lives in every way available to straight people. Queers have always had to live and love in a world whose emotional economy was designed by and for straight people, but now the pressure is on for everyone, particularly white, wealthy, urban LGBT people, to adopt the rituals of what writer and theorist Hannah Black calls 'the disaster of straightness'.[1]

The colonisation of love by capitalist patriarchy is a deeply painful thing. It means that structural sexism and cultural violence are played out on small, private stages, which is what makes them so very hard to recognise and resist.

Human love is radical, and it is devastating. And human love has been thoroughly captured by neoliberalism, by the mindset and mechanisms of profit.

THE LANGUAGE OF LOVE

Love is a gendered thing. It also makes life worth living and politics worth doing. Everyone seems to agree that love is important – but what sort of love?

Part of the problem is our lack of language to describe love, and that problem is political. Semantic context collapse means that we only have one word, 'love', for the vast spectrum of passion and compassion, compersion and care that make our species worth saving. The English language has hundreds of thousands of words, including many thousands of synonyms and not counting abbreviations and acronyms, but only one to describe the very thing we're told is most important. And of every possible definition of love, it is romantic love between couples, monogamous sexual and social commitment between two people that is considered the most important. This is no accident.

Love and fucking are the field on which gender gets personal. Where stereotypes are cast in craving and formed in bitterness on every side. The more I talk to people about love and work and gender and sex and power, the more it comes down to passion and loss, which in turn come down to the stories we tell ourselves and how they map on to our experience of real human beings trying to fit our messy, meaty hearts into the anatomically inaccurate totem of romance. And yet love, romantic love, is the one thing we're not supposed to question. Why not?

When we talk about love conquering all, when we speak, in that glazed, cultish way, of love's healing power, of its capacity to sweep away reason and save us from our cramped and depressing selves, we are not talking about love in its broadest sense. We are not referring to the actual practice of caring for a person and being cherished in return, or of giving of oneself for another, whether that be a friend, a family member, a lover or a stranger. The undirectional love lip-synched by pop starlets and garlanded in gaudy red misrepresentations of vital anatomy is not that love.

The notion of romance that we are all encouraged to go searching for is something different. It is something smaller and more specific. It is love as ritual and as product, love as an erotic object rather than a practice, love whose highest ideal is still heterosexual, monogamous romance leading eventually to lasting marriage. This sort of love is valued above every other, even though it is now a minority practice, and even though the many millions who are living happily in such partnerships find the reality far more complex than is considered proper to discuss.

It would help if we could distinguish this ideal of love, this grab-bag of twee, semi-sexual heteronormative romance rituals, from all the other potential kinds of love. To ease that process, I find it best to think of that narrow romantic fantasy in its proper place, as Love™.

Love™ is the other side of the pornographic narrative; the other side of Sex™. It is the story told in the light where the machinistic, vengeful clusterfuck of most straight porn is the story told in the dark, and the thing about stories is that somebody made them up.

The competing narratives of hypercompetitive patriarchal porn and fairy-tale for-ever romance are meant to be polar opposites. They are certainly almost never part of the same plot, outside the widely and unjustly ridiculed universe of cheap ladies' paperbacks. But there are some important similarities. Both stories, Love™ and Sex™, hold us up to impossible standards. Both demand that we see another person as less than human, merely a body filling a prewritten role in our script for romantic or erotic ecstasy. Both are wildly unrealistic, and both set us up to fail.

Back in the real world, most people's lives exist on a spectrum somewhere between One True Love and meaningless rutting. Even those of us taken in by the fantasy know this to be the case, and yet it's frowned upon to speak of that spectrum in positive terms. We are required instead to acknowledge that any person or pair of persons failing to achieve Love™ or Sex™ are doomed to live terribly sad lives, blue of gonad and broken-hearted.

EITHER WAY YOU'RE ON YOUR KNEES

In many social situations, it is now more acceptable to say you don't believe in God than it is to say you don't believe in love. Love™ has become devotional, especially for women. We search for it, profess belief in it, make sacrifices for it. Love™ is considered the passion besides which all others are inferior – especially for women, who are not permitted any greater love. 'To give proof,' as the Tiqqun collective observe, 'it would be enough to recall how, through the entire process of "civilisation", the criminalisation of all sorts of passions accompanied the sanctification of love as the one true passion.'[2]

The quest for Great Love is the ultimate devotion, the

ultimate sign of being a good woman who can command the interest of men. Some of us may have loosened the vice of religious misogyny, but we still find ourselves on our knees. Love™ demands demonstrations of faith in the face of logic. 'The perfect person is out there,' we say to our friends who are single and sad, as if merely repeating the mantra might make it so.

One of the most misunderstood lines by Karl Marx is the hoary old quote about religion being 'the opium of the masses'. This is usually taken to mean that religion is an intoxicant, a mug's game, and that people who fall for it are deluded. What Marx went on to say was that 'religious suffering is, at one and the same time, the expression of real suffering and a protest against real suffering. Religion is the sigh of the oppressed creature, the heart of a heartless world.' The thing about opium, you see, is that it isn't just addictive – at the time, as writer and theorist James Butler notes, 'opium was a medicine and comfort while also being a potent drug'. Religion, like opium, was a refuge from the anxieties of the age, replacing personal, individual despair with a whole new set of problems. Right now, romantic love as we know it functions in much the same way.

We don't just fall for all of this romantic faff because we're stupid, or gullible, or weak. We fall because we want to, because we need to believe that something will make the rest of our lives safe and meaningful. The postures of romance, particularly straight, married romance, allow us to reject the grim meat-hook reality of work and death even as they fashion us for it, pairing us off into little pockets of pain and passion: you and me against the world, baby. We fall in love because it's easier than learning to swim in the stuff.

Why must we 'fall' in love? Why must love be a lapse? Why can't it be better than that? Here I am, talking like a zealot, when what I really mean to say is just this: modern love is like finding yourself lost and starving on a street you don't know. You walk into a late-night grocery store with hunger boiling in the pit of your belly and find the shelves stacked with cupcakes, brightly coloured, sugar-sweet, perhaps with a cartoon smile painted on in frosting.

If you're lucky, cupcakes are just what you want. If you're unlucky, it's cupcakes or nothing. And even if you do want those cupcakes, because after all, cupcakes are what everyone's selling, that kind of sugar will make you crash hard if you don't keep eating it. So when the first cupcake is gone, you have another, and then another, as many cupcakes as you can buy, bingeing until you feel sick, until you never want to see another fucking cupcake again, but still you're terrified that without them you'll starve.

In her important book *All About Love*, bell hooks writes that:

> Now that . . . women are more economically independent, men who want to maintain dominance must deploy subtler strategies to colonise and disempower them. Even the wealthiest professional woman can be 'brought down' by being in a relationship where she longs to be loved and is consistently lied to.[3]

Women across the classes are taught to seek the love of men first, to assess our worth on the basis of how good we are at keeping and holding male attention. And across the classes, romantic humiliation can be used to bring women low. Every straight man I have ever spoken to about dating remains angrily convinced that women have all the power when it comes to romantic dealings, including the ultimate power: to accept or reject a man's sexual advances, to put men in the 'friend zone', which is a mug's game, because of course no real man would actually want to be a woman's friend. The power to say no to sex makes women monstrous to men, feels like more than a fitting exchange for every other sort of power denied to women and girls over these long, weary generations.

This is perfectly true, as long as one believes that the power to say no to sex is respected in practice. Men as a class are incensed by that process of female refusal. They rail against it, push against it, undermine it with violence. They come out in their cowardly thousands online to protest at the idea that sexual consent should be respected.

But men, too, have equal power of refusal in relationships. They can refuse to give of themselves in a way that is equally humiliating to women who have grown up learning that they were failing on a basic level if they could not command the love and commitment of men. And that's it. That's how heterosexuality makes us all miserable. That's the privatisation of love.

'Love' is one of those words, like 'Freedom', 'Security' and 'Democracy', that has been captured and tortured until it gives in to its polar opposite. Love is supposed to be the one thing you can't kill. And maybe that's true, if you come at it with a gun in your fist. But there are other things you can do to undermine the power of human passion. You can rip it away from kids and redeliver it processed and packaged in pink and blue cans for somebody else's profit, like powdered milk you pay for with your heart's blood. You can mangle it into a mode of production. You can use it to isolate people in antagonistic pairs and let them blame each other for the structural lack of sweetness in the world. You can privatise passion, annex affection. You can create the appearance of scarcity where there ought to be abundance. You can make the search for simple connection into a miserable, exhausting ritual that demands rigid gender conformity and represses the human spirit. And that's how you kill love.

LOVE IS WORK

Almost midnight outside an occupied university building. The sexual tension between me and one of the non-elected student leaders is so thick that we can hardly see each other through it. I'm mortified by how much I want him. This cocky, jockish young man keeps trying to beat me in discussions and failing, and people are asking me when the hook-up is going to happen. Like it's a done thing.

There's little privacy in an occupation, but we've found some, in the pool of dark outside the corridor by the dustbins. It's December and the air is bitter and the three beers we've had aren't enough to keep us warm. We lean a little closer.

And this is it, this is the moment where the music soars

and we make out messily under the moon and the credits roll. That doesn't happen. Instead, he says: 'I'm sorry. I'm really sorry. But I only kiss very beautiful girls.'

He's drunk. He doesn't mean to be that much of a prick. But we both know what he means, and it hurts because he's right: I'm not the sort of girl who gets kissed by boys like that. I'm not a sexy little package. I'm scrappy and opinionated. I'm devoted to my work and my politics. I keep my hair cut short and my clothes clashing and I wear big boots and don't dumb down. Attraction is only a part of it. Socially speaking, you do not put your mouth to a loaded gun.

I still feel like I've been dragged out and shot behind the dustbins.

And for a moment that spins out reeling in the hurt, private parts of the heart, I wish I was a different kind of girl. A girl like the girl I see the same boy rolling under a blanket with in the communal bedding area two hours later, soft-spoken with long, pretty hair. I am eaten up by jealousy, and that's how they get you. It's the night before a big march, but I abandon sleep.

Instead, I get the laptop out and take it to a place where people are too stoned and sleepy to take notice of my pathetic little tears. This is stupid. There's work to be done. Tomorrow tens of thousands of us are going to take to the streets to demand fair access to education, and my smashed little heart shouldn't matter. But it does. The whole world is changing, and I just want to be the kind of girl who gets taken in somebody's arms. In the corridor, some kids are training to resist police batons with makeshift cardboard armour, which is a great way to fuck yourself up the night before a big demo. I think about maybe growing my hair out and wearing more skirts.

And that's how they get you.

That's how they keep you in line. I have, from time to time, been threatened with violence for walking too proud and talking too much and wearing my hair like a robot rent-boy from the future, but those threats are easy to laugh off. But deep down, I know if I choose not to play the good girl game, I might not get as many kisses as I want. And that's so much more terrifying.

This, then, is how women are kept in line. The threat of violence is a fearful thing, but its injustice is clear, and there is always the risk of rebellion. To threaten someone with a slap, or a kick, with broken teeth or a split skull or rape or murder, is not always enough to keep them behaving as you would want them to behave for ever. To threaten someone with loss of love, however, is a violence far more profound and painful: there are few people who would choose a long, healthy life without love over a short, painful life full of it. To tell a person that if they don't do what they're told they will never be loved is an existential threat akin to soul-murder. 'If you do not do this, you will be beaten' is ultimately far less effective than 'if you do not do this, nobody will love you'.

It is that fear that keeps us cowed and conformist. It is the fear that we will be unloved.

We don't pare ourselves down and tart ourselves up and process our personality into the mould deemed most pleasing by mainstream culture because we're stupid, or cowardly. We do it because we fear loss of love. We do it because we grew up learning, unless our parents were particularly enlightened, that we were unworthy of love unless we conformed to a certain set of rules about how to look, dress and behave. Of course, they get you coming and going.

If you do follow all the rules, if you ever get it perfectly right, then, of course, you're a dull bimbo, a brainless fembot, just as unworthy of male respect as the ones who didn't. You're a cardboard cut-out girlfriend, and you can be dismissed. No woman is ever dismissable, but sometimes, if we want men to love us, we are forced to act dismissable – and don't all good girls want men to love them?

LOVE OBJECTS

There is a princess in all our heads: she must be destroyed. At the time of writing, the entire global press has been recruiting us all into the Cult of Kate Middleton for upwards of three years, and businesses are gleefully cashing in on young women's insatiable lust for princess paraphernalia. Fake tiaras and fashion handbooks play into the collective fantasy that one day, if you are beautiful and good enough, you too can marry the inbred great-great-grandchild of some bloodless aristocrat whose distant relations were better at murdering huge numbers of peasants than some other bloodless aristocrat.

As social mobility collapses, princess propaganda is enjoying a shocking pink renaissance, hooking grown women who should know better into the hoary old narrative of One True Love leading inexorably to titular rights to the Duchy of Lancaster. When we grow up, the princess becomes the shining girl, the good girlfriend. It may look less likely that we'll inherit Cornwall, but we can still be somebody else's beautiful sidekick, which is the best thing a girl can be.

We talk a lot about women as sex objects, but the reduction of women to love objects does just as much damage; it's a degradation more intimate and enduring. The love object is a thing to be desired and pitied all at once. She is the helpmeet, the saint, the fantasy. She is never a complete person. Whatever attributes make her interesting – maybe she can cook, or sew, or shoot a gun, or solve a crime – she exists ultimately for the hero's edification. She is nothing without him.

The notion of women as sex objects is understood. Just as many of us, however, spend our lives trying to mould ourselves into love objects. Almost every female protagonist, in every story written or designed by men, is a love object: a creature fabricated to fulfil a role in somebody else's grand narrative. The love object is always a supporting character, even when she gets the most screentime. She delights, she entices, she is slender and beautiful and whimsical and invariably poorly written, and so many of us spend a great deal of time trying to be her.

Stories shape us, even the shit ones. Even the ones that are simplistic and obviate a great deal of real-life experience by design. Stories are how we organise our lives, how we streamline our desires, and sometimes they fall short, and sometimes they disappoint us, and they always matter. For women, love stories are the stories we are allowed to cast ourselves in, and those are the stories that shape our cravings and identities.

We can be the sweet princess who needs rescuing. We can be the femme fatale, the trophy blonde or the shining girl who saves the brooding young hero from his suffering and helps him to believe in the beauty of life. Women learn that the only stories we really get to be the heroes of, from *Pride and Prejudice* to *The Matrix* to *Bridget Jones's Diary*, are love stories – and we don't even get to be the hero of those. Love™ is meant to be the overwhelming object of a woman's early life; her story ends when she finds it, or fails to find it. The most important thing is that her story ends.

Very occasionally, in romances and summer blockbusters, one runs across the man as love object, with floppy hair and flashing eyes where his personality should be, his only flaw being quite how besotted he is with our heroine. The shallowness of these two-dimensional beefcakes is immediately obvious: though their endings are invariably happy, few young men aspire to that role in real life, because they have so many other stories to work with. Why would a little boy choose to play the handsome prince when he can be a knight or a wizard, a hero or a villain, Superman or Batman? Little girls, though, only ever get two choices: we can be the princess, or we can be the witch. And everybody knows what happens to women who do their own magic. Stories matter. Girls trying to find their way in the world still learn that unless we play the love object, there are oven doors in our future.

This is why female artists and women writers remain figures of suspicion. Men are allowed to make their work, their practice, the central romance of their lives. Men are allowed to love their art, their writing, their passion, a little bit more than anything else. Women are not, and if we choose to do so anyway, we will always be seen as lacking something, or taking on a man's role, or both. Whatever else we do with our lives, we must carve out part of our hearts in the service of others, or we are not really women. We are permitted to be the wives and lovers of great men, but if we try to become great ourselves – even now, when there are fewer and fewer legal barriers stopping us from doing so – there must be something wrong with us. Sometimes you have to decide between doing what you love and being lovable, and the decision is always painful.

I WAS A MANIC PIXIE DREAM GIRL

Like scabies and syphilis, Manic Pixie Dream Girls were with us long before they were accurately named. It was the critic Nathan Rabin who coined the term in a review of the film *Elizabethtown*, explaining that the character of the Manic Pixie Dream Girl 'exists solely in the fevered imaginations of sensitive writer-directors to teach broodingly soulful young men to embrace life and its infinite mysteries and adventures'.[4] She pops up everywhere these days, in films and comics and novels and television, fascinating lonely geek dudes with her magical joie-de-vivre and boring the hell out of anybody who likes their women to exist in all three dimensions rather than two. She doesn't get a story. She is part of a story that happens to other people. That's what girls are supposed to be.

Men grow up expecting to be the hero of their own story. Women grow up expecting to be the supporting actress in somebody else's. As a kid growing up with books and films and stories instead of friends, that was always the narrative injustice that upset me more than anything else. I felt it sometimes like a sharp pain under the ribcage, the kind of chest pain that lasts for minutes and hours and might be nothing at all or might mean you're slowly dying of something mundane and awful. It's a feeling that hit when I understood how few girls got to go on adventures. I started reading science fiction and fantasy long before Harry Potter and *The Hunger Games*, before mainstream female leads very occasionally got more at the end of the story than together with the protagonist. Sure, there were tomboys and bad girls, but they were freaks and were usually killed off or married off quickly. Lady hobbits didn't bring the ring to Mordor. They stayed at home in the Shire.

In Doug Rushkoff's book *Present Shock*,[5] he discusses the phenomenon of 'narrative collapse': the idea that in the years between 11 September 2001 and the financial crash of 2008, all of the old stories about God and Duty and Money and Family and America and the Destiny of the West finally disintegrated, leaving us with fewer sustaining fairy tales to die for and even fewer to live for.

This is plausible, but future panic, like the future itself, is not evenly distributed. Not being sure what story you're in any more is a different experience depending on whether or not you were expecting to be the hero of that story. Women and girls, and low-status men, often don't have that expectation. We expect to be forgettable supporting characters, or sometimes, if we're lucky, attainable objects to be slung over the hero's shoulder and carried off at the end of the final page. The only way we get to be in stories is to be stories ourselves. If we want anything interesting at all to happen to us we have to be a story that happens to somebody else, and when you're a young girl looking for a script, there are a limited selection of roles to choose from.

Manic Pixies, like other female archetypes, crop up in real life partly because fiction creates real life, particularly for those of us who grow up immersed in it. Women behave in ways that they find sanctioned in stories written by men who know better, and men and women seek out friends and partners who remind them of a girl they met in a book one day when they were young and longing.

For me, Manic Pixie Dream Girl was the story that fit. Of course, I didn't think of it in those terms; all I saw was that in the books and series I loved – mainly science fiction, comics and offbeat literature, not the mainstream films that would later make the MPDG trope famous – there were certain kinds of girl you could be, and if you weren't a busty bombshell, if you were maybe a bit weird and clever and brunette, there was another option.

And that's how I became a Manic Pixie Dream Girl. The basic physical and personality traits were already there, and some of it was doubtless honed by that learned girlish desire to please – because the posture does please people, particularly the kind of sad, bright, bookish young men who have often been my friends and lovers. I had the raw materials: I'm five feet nothing, petite and small-featured with skin the colour of something left on the bottom of a pond for too long and messy hair that's sometimes dyed a shocking shade of red or pink. At least, it was before I washed all the dye out last year, partly to stop soulful Zach-Braff-a-likes following me to the shops.

And, yes, I'm a bit strange and sensitive and daydreamy, and, yes, I retain a somewhat embarrassing belief in the ultimate decency of humanity and the transformative brilliance of music, although I'm ambivalent on the Shins. I love to dance, I play the guitar badly, and I also – since we're in confession mode, dear reader, hear and forgive – I also play the fucking ukulele. Truly. But the Manic Pixie is never a point-of-view character, and she isn't understood from the inside. She's one of those female tropes who is permitted precisely no interiority. Instead of a personality, she has eccentricities, a vaguely offbeat favourite band, a funky fringe.

Most of the classic Manic Pixie Dream Girls claim to be ironic re-imaginings of a character trope that they fail to actually interrogate in any way. Irony is, of course, the last vestige of modern crypto-misogyny: all those lazy stereotypes and hurtful put-downs are definitely a joke, right up until they aren't, and clearly you need a man to tell you when and if you're supposed to take sexism seriously.

One of these soi-disant ironic films is *(500) Days of Summer*, the opening credits of which refer to the real-world heartbreak on which writer-director Scott Neustadter based the character of Summer: 'Any resemblance to people living or dead is purely coincidental. Especially you, Jenny Beckman. Bitch.'[6]

Men write women, and they rewrite us, for revenge. It's about obsession, and control. Perhaps the most interesting of the classics, then, is the recent *Ruby Sparks*, written by a woman, Zoe Kazan, who also stars as the title character. It's all about a frustrated young author who writes himself a perfect girlfriend, only to have her come to life. When she inevitably proves more difficult to handle in reality than she did in his fantasy, the writer's brother comments: 'You've written a girl, not a person.'

'I think defining a girl and making her lovable because of her music taste or because she wears cute clothes is a really superficial way of looking at women. I did want to address that,' Kazan told the *Huffington Post*. 'Everybody is setting out to write a full character. It's just that some people are limited in their imagination of a girl.'[7]

Those imaginative limits, that failure of narrative, is imposed off the page, too, in the most personal of ways. I stopped being a Manic Pixie Dream Girl around about the time I got rid of the last vestiges of my eating disorder and knuckled down to a career. It's so much easier, if you have the option, to be a girl, not a person. It's definitely easier to be a girl than it is to do the work of being a grown woman, especially when you know that grown women are far more fearful to the men whose approval seems so vital to your happiness. And yet something in me was rebelling against the idea of being a character in somebody else's story. I wanted to write my own.

I became successful, or at least modestly so – and that changed how I was perceived, entirely and all at once. I was no longer That Girl. I didn't have time to save boys any more. I had other priorities, and those priorities included writing. You cannot be a writer and have writing be anything other than the central romance of your life, which is one thing they don't tell you about being a woman writer: it's its own flavour of lonely. Men can get away with loving writing a little bit more than anything else. Women can't: our partners and, eventually, our children are expected to take priority. Even worse, I wasn't writing poems or children's stories, I was writing reports, political columns. I've recently been experimenting with answering 'fashion' rather than 'politics' when men casually ask me what I write about, and the result has been a 100 per cent increase in phone numbers, business cards and offers of drinks. This is still substantially fewer advances than I received when I gave the truthful answer that what I wrote was: 'sometimes, in notebooks, just for myself'.

Lately, though, as I've been working on longer ideas about sexism and class and power, I keep coming back to love, to the meat and intimacy of fucking and how it so often leads so treacherously to kissing. I was prepared for the personal to be political. What I didn't understand until quite recently was that the political can be so, so personal.

There was never a moment in my life when I decided to be a writer. I can't remember a time when I didn't know for sure that that's what I'd do, in some form, and for ever. But there have been times when I didn't write, because I was too depressed or anxious or running away from something, and those times have coincided almost precisely with the occasions when I had most sexual attention from men. I wish I'd known, at twenty-one, when I made up my mind to try to write seriously for a living if I could, that that decision would also mean a choice to be intimidating to the men I fancied, a choice to be less attractive, a choice to stop being That Girl and start becoming a grown woman, which is the worst possible thing a girl can do, which is why so many of those Manic Pixie Dream Girl characters, as written by male geeks and scriptwriters, either die tragically young or are somehow immortally fixed at the physical and mental age of nineteen and a half. Meanwhile, in the real world, the very worst thing about being a real-life MPDG is the look of disappointment on the face of someone you really care about when they find out you're not their fantasy at all – you're a real human who breaks wind and has a job.

If I'd known what women have to sacrifice in order to write, I would not have allowed myself to be so badly hurt when boys whose work and writing I found so fascinating found those same qualities threatening in me. I would have understood what Kate Zambreno means when she says, in her marvellous book *Heroines*,[8] I do not want to be an ugly woman, and when I write, I am an ugly woman. I would have been less surprised when men encouraged me to be politer and grow my hair long even as I helped them out with their own media careers. My Facebook feed is full of young male writers who I have encouraged to believe in themselves, set up with contacts, taken on adventures and talked into the night about the meaning of journalism with, who are now in long-term relationships with people who are content to be That Girl. I would have understood quite clearly what I was choosing when I chose, sometime around the time I packed two suitcases and walked out on Garden State Boy, to be a person who writes her own stories, rather than a story that happens to other people.

I try hard, now, around the men in my life, to be as unmanic, as unpixie and as resolutely real as possible, because I don't want to give the wrong impression.

And it's a struggle. Because I remain a small, friendly, excitable person who wears witchy colours and has a tendency towards the twee. I still know that if I wanted to, I could attract one of those lost, pretty nerd boys I have such a weakness for by dialling up the twee and dialling down the smart, just as I know that the hurt in their eyes when they realise you're a real person is not something I ever want to see again. I still love to up sticks and go on adventures, but I no longer drag mournful men-children behind me when I do, because it's frankly exhausting. I still play the ukulele. I wasn't kidding about the fucking ukulele. But I refuse to burn my energy adding extra magic and sparkle to other people's lives to get them to love me. I'm busy casting spells for myself. Everyone who was ever told a fairy tale knows what happens to women who do their own magic.

So here's what I've learned, in twenty-seven years of reading books and kissing boys. Firstly, averagely pretty white women in their late teens and twenties are not the biggest, most profoundly unsolvable mystery in the universe. Trust me. I should know. Those of us with an ounce of lust for life are almost universally less interesting than we will be in our thirties and forties. The one abiding secret about us is that we're not fantasies, and we weren't made to save you: we're real people, with flaws and cracked personalities and big dreams and digestive tracts. It's no actual mystery, but it remains a fact that the half of the human race with a tendency to daydream about a submissive, exploitable, transcendent ideal of the other seems perversely unwilling to discover.

Secondly, you can spend your whole life being a story that happens to somebody else. You can twist and cram and shave down every aspect of your personality that doesn't quite fit into the story boys have grown up expecting, but eventually, one day, you'll wake up and want something else, and you'll have to choose.

Because the other thing about stories is that they end. The book closes, and you're left with yourself, a grown fucking woman with no more pieces of cultural detritus from which to construct a personality. I tried and failed to be a character in a story somebody else had written for me. What concerns me now is the creation of new narratives, the opening of space in the collective imagination for women who have not been permitted such space before, for women who don't exist to please, to delight, to attract men, for women who have more on our minds. Writing is a different kind of magic, and everyone knows what happens to women who do their own magic – but it's a risk you have to take.

LOVE (:) YOUR JOB

Under late capitalism, love has become like everything else: a prize to be won, an object to be attained, a commodity to be hoarded until it loses value or can be traded up for a better bargain. On the other hand, if we are to believe the truly staggering amount of pop propaganda on offer, Love™ is also something that is, by its very nature, free – something that must absolutely never involve money or value exchange of any kind, if it is to be deemed 'true' love.

The insistence that Love Always Comes Free – that Love™ cannot ever be related to money or value exchange – is remarkably convenient. Because it turns out that Love™ is also the theoretical basis for most of the work done for free, largely by women, so that the mechanisms of profit and production can be maintained. Most of the work of child-care, cooking, cleaning, personal care, helpmeeting and mopping up your husband's ego after a hard day's wage labour is not recognised as 'real work' because it is done out of 'love' – and if love workers ever questioned their conditions, their love would automatically be less worthwhile, less genuine, than the love of all those girlfriends, wives, mothers and daughters who do their duty with a silent smile and a bottle of Valium in the bottom drawer.

Love can also be work. Love is, in fact, difficult and challenging as well as rewarding, and even at its most exciting is deeply involved with money. I'm not trying to argue that childcare, housework and the work of supporting partners through waged labour should necessarily be paid, although if I did, I wouldn't be the first to do so. It is important, however, to recognise that a lot of the work that women do remains unpaid or underpaid because we think of it as 'love', as a moral expression of feeling rather than a practical task of immense and tangible value. A lot of that 'second shift' of caretaking that is worth untold billions every year and is still performed largely by women, is exempted from consideration and left undiscussed precisely because it is understood as 'love', and 'love' always comes for free.[9] A good job it does, because if it didn't there'd be a hell of a bill to pay.

For men, Love™ does not mean work in the same way that it traditionally has done for women. For men, Love™ is more likely to mean continuing in one's occupation of choice with the support of a partner who cherishes and believes in you, will take care of you when work exhausts you, will handle all the arrangements for the care and upbringing of your children so you don't have to think about it, and will provide you with your preferred form of sexual release at the end of the working day. The fact that this is a fantasy doesn't stop it standing in the way of real progress on the domestic front and making a lot of men and women miserable along the way.

There are a growing number of men who have come to shoulder a portion of the domestic burden, and even a minority who work as primary carers for children, but that minority is still small – and enormously culturally under-represented to the extent that such arrangements still fail to register in the life plans of most young men. The weary narrative of the 'male provider' or 'breadwinner' continues to be a source of anxiety for a great many men despite having little historical basis in fact, there having been very few historical moments when women's work has been confined solely to the home. Nonetheless, for men the boundaries between love and work are clearly drawn. For men, love is supposed to be the reward you get in return for work; for women, love is work in itself.

Marriage used to be understood as an essentially economic arrangement. In this age of Disney Princesses and One True

Lovers, marriage is still an economic arrangement, and one that is beneficial to any state whose wealth is based on property ownership, as evidenced by the panicked efforts of successive government to formalise and reward it within the tax system. That's one reason why even those queer people opposed to marriage on principle nonetheless insist on their right to ruin their lives on the same way straight people have been able to for centuries: because there's money at stake.

Online dating has brought a lot of joy to a lot of lonely people – between 20 and 35 per cent of new relationships now begin on the Internet – but it has also formalised the similarity between one's professional and romantic CVs. In many cases the only way you can tell if a person is applying for a role in the back office or your bedroom is whether or not they have included a picture of themselves drunk at a festival riding an inflatable alligator to prove that they like 'having fun'. You tell your potential boyfriend the same lies you tell your potential boss: I'm easy-going, flexible, low-stress and cheerful, just like you want me to be.

Love is supposed to be what makes us human. Why, then, is what we so commonly think of as love so easy for machines to imitate? Valentine-bots are programmed to stalk online dating sites scamming desperate people – often but not exclusively women – by going through the motions of passion. Romance is many things, but it is not a Turing test: its language and rituals are so well understood that a simple computer programme can imitate them quite easily.

If love is becoming more like a job, with schedules, interviews and promotion grades, then it is certainly the case that work is becoming much more like romance. Social scientists now speak seriously of 'emotional labour' – the elements of customer service, people-pleasing and ritual soothing of egos that are now part of the daily routine of most bullshit jobs. Bosses don't just want a job of work done: they want you to smile while you're doing it.

There's another important way in which romantic love has become like work under neoliberalism: it is at once all-consuming and precarious. You are expected to pour the whole of your energy, all of your passion, time and enthusiasm into one endeavour, even though you know that it could end at any time if the magic disappears, or the economy tanks.

Our expectations of love and marriage have become ever loftier even as lifelong partnership ceases to be the norm: a recent study[10] showed that where once one could at least acknowledge that a romantic life partnership was about expediency, sharing the bills and having someone on hand to put up shelves, now the things that we expect from marriage are more abstract and urgent: true kinship, decades of erotic fulfilment and a sense of spiritual completeness.

Even as our expectations of Love™ become more frantic, the pressure is on for this ideal bond to replace the human kindness confiscated by the world of work. The purpose of dating, as far as the market is concerned, is to produce households. We are sectioned off into couples in order to make the production and reproduction of 'human capital' easier – self-reproducing family units isolated in their own struggle. Romantic love is both the consolation and respite from the privations of work and the means of making that work sustainable.

Women, in and out of romantic relationships, carry the burden of emotional labour. We do the work of healing and mending that we have always done.

Under late capitalism almost all of us are damaged goods, but it is women who end up trying to fix that damage, or at least keep the gears greased so the machine carries on functioning. I see so many bright, brilliant women pouring their energy into salving the hurt of men who cannot turn to each other for comfort. We do it as sisters, as mothers, as friends, and especially as lovers and wives, because of the sheer number of men and boys who are socialised out of intimacy with anyone they're not fucking.

We pay with our time, with our emotional energy, with our attention and care, because that's what women do, and that's what love is: trying to carry another person's pain and stress, even if they resent you for it, which they frequently do. As I said earlier, you can't save the world one man at a time. That doesn't stop many of us trying.

Thirty years ago, it was common for women to be expected to do the washing up after any gathering as a matter of course. Now we're stuck cleaning up the emotional messes of modern life – and late capitalism has left us with an unending stack of dirty dishes. A great many of the brightest and bravest women I know are constantly soaped to the elbow in the gunk of men's silent distress. This would be hard enough if we didn't have our own shit to deal with.

As work and housing become more precarious, as it becomes more normal to move hundreds of miles to find employment, and as ties of geographic community are eroded by austerity, romantic partnership is now expected to provide the main source of emotional as well as economic support. As Richard Kim and Lisa Duggan note in their seminal article 'Beyond Gay Marriage'[11] romantic love and marriage are now expected to do more even as 'the net effect of the neoliberal economic policies imposed in recent decades has been to push economic and social responsibility away from employers and government and onto private households. The stress on households is intensifying, as people try to do more with less . . . In more and more cases, the sole remaining resource is the cooperative, mutually supporting household or kinship network. But if marriage is the symbolic and legal anchor for households and kinship networks, and marriage is increasingly unstable, how reliable will that source of support be?'

In her book *Against Love*, Laura Kipnis notes that 'the conditions of lovability are remarkably convergent with those of a cowed workforce and a docile electorate . . . how very convenient that we're so willing to police ourselves and those we love, and call it living Happily Ever After.' Fear of loss of love makes us hesitate. It chokes the impulse to freedom at the back of the throat before it is spoken. If we have to behave in order to be loved, if we cannot be fulfilled without it, of course we will do whatever it takes to make love happen – even at the cost of our personhood.

Your job is now your boyfriend: neither of them can be trusted to stick around, so you'd better make sure they know how much you love them. You have to be passionate about your work, even if your work is lining up packets of pasta shapes on a shelf. You have to pretend that you dreamed of pasta arrangement as a child; that all you've ever wanted is to stack carbohydrate staples in a supermarket, and even though you and your line manager both know it's not true, you've got to say the words and hold the smile. You must love your job so much that if you weren't getting paid, you'd do it for free: all waged labour has become the Girlfriend Experience.

LOVE AND OTHER ADVENTURES

Is there any more pitiable creature than the single woman? Samhita Mukhopadhyay, writing in her book *Outdated*, fears not: 'When she is not the stereotypical bubblegum popular culture notion of the "single gal about town", she is at her most reviled and feared: on welfare, representative of the failure of femininity, a threat to masculinity, a threat to the family, a spinster, a cat lady, bitter, alone, jealous, never been kissed, and I could go on.'[12] The reality remains that 'Women who do it on their own bear the financial, social and emotional cost of being single in a society unwilling to truly support their lives.'[13] Women learn to fear being 'left on the shelf', to associate it with poverty and isolation.

We are all encouraged to feel sorry for ourselves if we are single, to consider ourselves incomplete, but women in particular are urged to consider themselves inferior if their time is not spent comforting and cosseting a man, and ideally children too. I have been single, in the strictest sense of the word, for some years, and although I haven't been encumbered by children, I have found it a marvellous adventure.

In 2011, the summer of rage and riots, I kiss a girl and she tastes of cigarettes and gin and I like it. She says she wants to be a mistress for ever. We met because we were sleeping with the same boy, and he isn't entirely comfortable with how close we've become. I buy her a cupcake from a posh sex shop. The cupcake has icing on it shaped like a cunt with a little clear sugar glaze trickling obscenely off the frosting folds. She laughs and eats it right there in front of me because she is hungry.

And then months later, on my balcony in late summer with tea and fags and ripped tights like dirty old ladies in training, I tell her that I want us all to be together. I love her and I love him and I love seeing them together, and when it's just the two of us we share something he isn't allowed to see, something private. We met at a protest, me pinching one of her cigarettes, which was and still is my way of telling her I need her. We're not the marrying kind. But he – he says no. He says we can't do it, it doesn't work with three, even though that's the only way it's ever worked between us. It's against the rules.

It ends like this: he yells at me and I leave him and I call her and cry and she tells me it's going to be okay. In cafés after work I ball up my fists, distracted, email her with everyday existential crises in the hope they're not fucking each other, left out, my legs crossed, missing his touch, missing her touch. Then he's sick of us both, and so we go out like we have before, eyeliner and cigarettes and bus passes on our way to corrupt young minds and stir the strange clutch of numbness in our chests, the place where the heart muscles don't seem to move. We are a tag team, an unstoppable perversion: we drag strange little hipsters into strange beds, turn them on to roll-ups and feminism. It's true love, not the way they tell it in stories, but it's still true.

Older now, months older, falling leaves and sleet and

7 a.m. on what has just ceased to be the night bus home through Angel, grey light creeping in under the curtain of a heady night and pushing its ice-cold fingers under the skin, unshowered and sleepless, sticky with sweat. I'm in the suicide seat, on the top deck at the front with the city rushing by underneath. My phone still has a couple of bars of charge, and I take it out to text one of the boys I left sleeping on the floor of a squat already miles behind me, miles away.

Checking in to my work emails, replying to my editor with fingers stiff from cold, I hollow out a little home under my heart for the shame which just isn't coming. Instead, I'm storing up this memory for future use.

Love™ is not true love, in the sense that many other kinds of love are also true. I have spent more time than I care to contemplate in my nimble years in the company of polyamorists, queer non-monogamists and the sort of people who prefer labels like 'love anarchists', which tends to mean that they have a zine collection and don't shave, which in its own way is wonderful. I have been in and witnessed enough non-monogamous relationships to know that different ways of organising love are not just possible, but essential – and they are also not the answer.

It's not that I don't believe in romantic love, in Love™. It patently exists. People shape their lives to stories, and sometimes it works. There are those out there for whom only the girl they knew in sixth-form French or the boy they met in the back of the squelchy indie disco will ever do, and no other relationship can possibly compare. I know couples like that, and I'm happy for them.

But the relatively recent cultural narrative of The One – the idea that everyone has a soulmate whom they are destined to love for ever, and that your life will always be incomplete if you fail to meet, mate and move in with that person – that's not just implausible, it's cruel. It implies that those who do not find their One will somehow never be complete, that those who divorce, who live and raise children alone, or who find alternative arrangements for happiness, have somehow failed as human beings. To my mind, that's a decidedly unromantic idea.

The gap between passionate, everlasting, all-consuming romance and meaningless rutting remains relatively unexplored by the publishing and film industries but, to paraphrase John Lennon, a great many people live in that gap. In real life, there is a superabundance of romance, friendship, partnership, sex and adventure to be had, and the truly terrible thing about shop-bought love in pretty packages is that it makes it seem that human feeling is a scarce resource. Which is just another reason why neoliberalism ruins everything.

In real life, human love is not a scarce resource. I don't mean to advocate casual sex, housing collectives and late nights drinking bad vodka with bisexual activists as alternatives that necessarily work for everyone, though they've always done so for me. The point is that the three Ms – marriage, mortgage and monogamy – do not work for everyone, either, and there's no reason why they should.

The people for whom Love™ works – and I really feel as if saying this might get me shot with heart-tipped Tasers by the love police – are in the minority. Now that we are not obliged to choose between celibate loneliness and yoking ourselves for ever to a person we may grow to despise, most people's lives contain many important relationships, and sometimes those relationships fade or fizzle out. That may not fit in with the dominant ideology – that monogamous marriage is the only possible healthy way to live, love and distribute welfare benefits – but it's a more accurate map of the human heart, which is not a cartoon symbol, but a complicated tangle of meat and blood.

The generation currently reaching adulthood in Europe and America is the first generation whose parents are as likely to have been divorced as they are to have been married or cohabiting.[14] Being raised by a married couple is no longer the norm.[15] No wonder increasing numbers of young people are exploring other options – polyamory, open relationships, extended circles of chosen family and fuckbuddies – and doing so in a way that's fundamentally different to the free love experiments of the past. It's as much about ethics as it is about drug-addled fuckfests though these are pleasant in their proper place.

Me, I believe in monogamy in much the same way as I believe in, say, cheese on toast. I'll eat it, but only for very special people, and not for every meal. There are other interesting and delicious toast options out there, and I support people's right to investigate those options without being punished.

Non-monogamy is not the same as fucking around, and neither of those things are essential to freedom in love. The idea of 'free love' has become bastardised by post-hippy clichés, by the enduring image of 1960s counterculture chauvinists with open shirts and flowers in their hair trying to wheedle women into bed without worrying about commitment. That's not what free love means. Free love is love that is not co-opted or coerced, love that is not mutually oppressive, love that is not another word for work, duty and conformity.

If we want love to be free, and if we want women to be free, we have to refuse to define ourselves by romantic love, by Love™, or lack of it. The power of the neoliberal notion of romantic love is such that it is almost a century since feminists routinely questioned its omnipotence, but today's growing girls of every age might do well to recall the words of Alexandra Kollontai:

> I still belong to the generation of women who grew up at a turning point in history. Love still played a very great role in my life. An all-too-great role! We, the women of the past generation, did not yet understand how to be free. The whole thing was an absolutely incredible squandering of our mental energy, a diminution of our labour power.
>
> . . . As great as was my love for my husband, immediately it transgressed a certain limit in relation to my feminine proneness to make sacrifice, rebellion flared in me anew. I had to go away, I had to break with the man of my choice, otherwise I would have exposed myself to the danger of losing my selfhood.[16]

FELLOW PRISONERS

Love has meant conformity for so long that we have forgotten that it also means defiance. Passion and compassion. Eros and philos. Seditious drinks and breathless texts and the sound of your heart hammering through your ribs at three in the morning. Aren't they what we clutch to ourselves when everything else falls away?

Some days, all I write is love letters. To friends and partners and boys I fucked once in a badly lit hotel in a strange city and have never seen again. I write love letters in ten-word Twitter messages and twenty-page emails. I write them in real time, one-handed, frantic, making up stories for men hundreds of miles away, putting down memories for girls I will hold in my heart for ever. The more weary I become of romance as commodity, the more love letters I send.

I began to really pay attention to the art of writing love letters when I first started sending handwritten mail to friends in prison. Then I received a letter of my own, telling me to read the essay 'Fellow Prisoners' by John Berger. Berger writes that:

> The prison is now as large as the planet and its allotted zones can vary and can be termed worksite, refugee camp, shopping mall, periphery, ghetto, office block, favela, suburb. What is essential is that those incarcerated in these zones are fellow prisoners. Cells have walls that touch across the world.
> [...] Liberty is slowly being found not outside but in the depths of the prison.[17]

If we are all fellow prisoners, every word we write is a prison letter, a missive to a soul in an adjacent cell, who may be a stranger or the best lover I ever knew. Keep your head high, and they won't win.

We get to choose what passions to censor, what sort of conformity we are prepared to conform. They can take a great deal from us, but not this. Money and hegemony and the disaster of neoliberal heterosexuality may have brought us to a point where it is nearly impossible for men and women and everyone else to love each other honestly, but it is only nearly impossible. It's not too late.

Women and girls in particular must summon the courage to devote the best efforts of our lives to something other than Love™. The idea that we have no control over who we love and what we do about it is one of the most disempowering things girls are ever told. Loneliness is a fearful thing. But a life lived grasping for another person to make you whole is just as fearful. If you see yourself as incomplete without a partner to be your 'other half', you will always be lonely, even in a partnership. It took me twenty-seven years to truly understand that just because you would give up every dream you ever had to see one special person smile doesn't mean you should.

I have been In Love™. I have fallen hard and fast for people with whom I shared something precious and unspeakable that went far beyond sex. I crossed continents, kicked in jobs and boarded trains in the middle of the night with all my hopes and some spare pairs of pants packed in a trundle-bag to be with those people. I pared down the awkward, ugly parts of my personality because I thought it might please them. I even felt, for brief moments, like the shining girl I knew I was supposed to be. I felt beautiful and special and treasured and I did my very best to make the other person feel that way too. It was fantastic. But after a while, it was also stifling.

Being In Love is great, but it's not the greatest happiness I have ever known. If I'm honest, I prefer plotting revolution with my friends. Every time I have been in that kind of love, I have ended up running, packing up my things and leaving notes real or imaginary and moving on, because I was sick of being a love object. And in that running, what I found was that outside fairy tales, love happens all the time.

Love is not a scarce resource. Love is not a prize to be won and jealously hoarded. Love is not a productive field, a sphere of work. Human love may have been colonised and appropriated by the demands of labour and capital, but it can be retaken. In 1910, the philosopher Emma Goldman wrote:

> Man has subdued bodies, but all the power on earth has been unable to subdue love. Man has conquered whole nations, but all his armies could not conquer love. Man has chained and fettered the spirit, but he has been utterly helpless before love . . . Yes, love is free; it can dwell in no other atmosphere. In freedom it gives itself unreservedly, abundantly, completely. All the laws on the statutes, all the courts in the universe, cannot tear it from the soil, once love has taken root.[18]

Beyond Happily Ever After, outside the single story of how life, work and partnership ought to be, love has always been free. When the fairy tale ends, the pages are still turning in the long, hard saga of human love, and there is always another story left to tell.

Afterword

People wanted me to sum up this book, to tie it up neatly with a set of answers. What programme, what policy would make life under neoliberalism less demeaning for women, queer people and their allies? At the Occupy protests, during the spring uprisings around the world, we were asked again and again what our demands were, so that they could be dismissed. Our first demand was not to be forced to engage on those terms. We did not want to be invited on to their panel shows or to the bottom of their ballot boxes. We refused the politics of the soundbite. We knew there were no easy answers.

Revolution begins in the human imagination. They can come for us with clubs and dogs but as long as we continue to dream of different ways to live, different ways to love and fight and grow old together, they will not win. There is power in the communities built by exiles and outcasts. There is power in the societies of broken kids growing up to change the world, and when it comes down to it we are all broken kids, fucked-up girls and lost boys just waiting to be found. We find each other in the unwatched spaces, the secret places, for as long as they last. We have the tools to build a better world in the wreck of the old one.

Feminism is one of those tools. Gender oppression is part of a structure of social control grinding us all down, keeping us docile, making sure that men and women everywhere question power as little as possible.

If we want to escape the straitjacket of gender under neoliberalism, we must stop trying so hard to hold ourselves and others up to impossible standards, standards we didn't set ourselves. We have to resist the schooled inner voice telling us to be good girls, tough boys, perfect women, strong men. If we are to realise a greater collective humanity, we must learn to see one another as human beings first.

The raw humanity of others is the unspeakable truth every mechanism of modern sexism is designed to disguise. If we have the courage to claim it, a change in consciousness is coming that will bring sexual and social revolution, that will free us to live and love more fully, and it will be as exactly as terrifying as it sounds.

That change in consciousness is coming from below. It's going to be led by women and queers and outsiders and their allies. It's going to come from ugly girls. Fat girls. Girls who aren't thin enough, rich enough, white enough. Girls with thick thighs and bellies that wobble and voices that carry – that resonate. Girls who are fucking angry. Girls who fuck for money. Old women. Trans women. Single mothers. Low-paid workers. Sex workers. There are so many ways to fall off the plinth patriarchy erects for the ideal woman. Eventually you're going to have to decide if you're going to wait to fall, or if you're going to jump.

Here are the worst things you can call a woman: ugly. Slutty. Fat. Bitter. Bitch. Cunt. The worst thing anyone can say to a woman, in short, is that she doesn't please you. We must get used to giving the answer: is that all you've got?

I have always found comrades in those who helped each other answer back.

This is still a violent, bigoted world, a world of neoliberal patriarchy that loves to make you hate yourself, especially if you're young, or poor, or weird, or a woman. To make you hurt yourself. To make you police the behaviour of others so that they remain as cowed as you feel. To cope with the intimate terrorism of neoliberal patriarchy we've got to work on giving fewer fucks. We've got to work on having no shame because we need no shame, because none of us do, unless we have hurt another person. We must be comfortable with knowing too much, but never knowing our place.

We've got to stop letting stale old men define our dreams. We must refuse to be ashamed of our desires, of our ambition, of our energy. We must refuse to judge others by any standard other than that of kindness and decency. We must not start out by apologising for all that we are.

It's about saying no and expecting that no to be respected. It's is about owning your own capacity to consent, and exercising it actively, again and again – not just in sexual terms but in political terms, too.

Because when we are done hating ourselves and hurting each other, we can get on with asking for what should be ours by right.

Neoliberal patriarchy gives us choice, but not freedom. No choice in an unfree society can be a truly free choice. The choice between this boss and that, the choice between marriage and penury, the choice between shame and self-denial, the choice between degrading work and debilitating poverty, all of these choices are meaningful, but they are not the same as liberty. Feminism and radical politics are about demanding more than a choice between one type of servitude and another. They are about insisting on our right to live with dignity, our right to shelter and sustenance and learning and the means to take care of one another.

I'm writing this on New Year's Day. This was a factory once. The gusty old warehouse where I'm living has been gutted and fitted with makeshift heaters and now eight queer kids live here, plus a rolling population of homeless activists, stray girlfriends and travelling refugees from the London rent crisis. In the empty offices, somebody has put in bedrooms, a kitchen, a cooker. The water is boiling for tea. Around me the sound of breathing swells and stills. People have laid down sleeping bags amongst nests of cables. This is our factory now.

I sit cross-legged like an urchin on top of my red suitcase. I have scattered its contents across two continents, on the floors of squats and artists' lofts and hotels and strangers' apartments, under tarpaulin at occupations and in the dressing rooms of cabaret shows. Every time I think I've found a place to unpack, my heart goes hunting for something new. And every time I lose hope, I find more of these places. Spaces where those who have found themselves exiled from the world of good behaviour by choice or circumstance live together in something like freedom for as long as they're allowed. Here we are, down and out in the global village. Around me in the quiet euphoria of the morning, sleeping young people are breathing in and out, drunk and dreaming. It's really easy to feel that you are dreaming alone. In a world where the powerful have little to fear except collective resistance, it is easy to feel that you are the only one who wants to live differently. Freedom can be a fearful thing. Wanting it can make you feel crazy.

But we have the technology now. We have the tools to liberate us from the privations of biology and the means to communicate without the mediation of the powerful and their paid mouthpieces. We have the technology to speak back to power not just in one voice, but in many.

A time is approaching when the humanity of women and girls and queer people and our allies will be understood in practice rather than acknowledged in passing. I believe that together we will find the courage to rewrite the old, tired scripts of work and power and sex and love, the old stories about what it means to be a beautiful woman, a strong man, a decent human being. I believe that the time is coming when those stories will be heard in numbers too big to silence. The great rewriting is already under way. Close your eyes. Turn the page. Begin.

Notes

INTRODUCTION

1 For this reading of neoliberal ideology I am indebted to Richard Seymour's analysis in *Against Austerity*, Pluto Press, London, 2014.

2 Valentine M. Moghadam, SHS/HRS/GED, 'The Feminization of Poverty', UNESCO, July 2005, http://www.cpahq.org/cpahq/cpadocs/Feminization_of_Poverty.pdf

3 See Natasha Walter, *The New Feminism* (London: Virago, 1999, new edn); see also Sarah Jaffe, 'Trickle Down Feminism', *Dissent*, winter 2013.

4 Object! Campaign in the UK and the campaigning of German feminist Alice Schwartzer; and many more.

5 In the words of Foster Friess, a major Republican donor during the 2012 US presidential elections: 'You know, back in my days, they used Bayer aspirin for contraception. The gals put it between their knees, and it wasn't that costly.' http://www.politico.com/blogs/burns-haberman/2012/02/foster-friess-in-my-day-gals-put-aspirin-between-their-114730.html

6 Nina Power in her excellent study *One Dimensional Woman*, Zero Books, London, 2009, calls this 'Feminism™'.

7 Cissexual or 'cis' means 'not transsexual or transgender'; 'cis' is to 'trans' as 'straight' is to 'gay' and, of course, a good many people fall somewhere in between.

8 This statement originated by Carol Hanisch in a paper of the same

name in the journal *Notes from the Second Year: Women's Liberation* 1970.

9 Sarah Menkedick, *It's Not Personal*, http://velamag.com/blog/its-not-personal

10 Quinn Norton deserves credit for this phrase. See 'Feminism's Twist Ending: Women and the Internet: Part Four', https://medium.com/ladybits-on-medium/e057ed6bb9e0 9Feminism's Twist Ending, 30 November 2013.

11 http://www.who.int/gender/documents/en/whopaper6.pdf

12 Catherine Hakim, *Honey Money: The Power of Erotic Capital*, Allen Lane, London, 2011.

13 Francis Fukuyama's book *The End of History and the Last Man*, Free Press, New York, 1992, is based on his essay 'The End of History?' written in response to the end of the Cold War and published in The National Interest in 1989.

CHAPTER 1: FUCKED-UP GIRLS

1 http://www.gallup.com/poll/158417/poverty-comes-depression-illness.aspx?utm_source=alert&utm_medium=email&utm_campaign=syndication&utm_content=morelink&utm_term=USA%20-%20Weight%20-%20Wellbeing%20-%20Well-Being%20Index

2 See Adjustment disorder, *DSM5*, American Psychiatric Publishing, Arlington, 2013.

3 See Marya Hornbacher, *Wasted*, Flamingo, London, 1999, and Lynn Ruth Miller, *Starving Hearts*, Excentrix Press, 2000.

4 http://www.theguardian.com/commentisfree/2014/jan/31/education-gender-gap-girls-schools-university

5 https://www.carlsonschool.umn.edu/.../GetFil...

6 http://www.spectator.co.uk/features/5244693/harriet-harman-is-either-thick-or-criminally-disingenuous/

7 http://news.bbc.co.uk/1/hi/uk_politics/8255909.stm

8 RuPaul: 'You're born naked. The rest is drag.' https://www.goodreads.com/quotes/218170-we-re-born-naked-and-the-rest-is-drag, from the autobiography *Lettin It All Hang Out*, Sphere, London, 1995.

9 www.Andred.com/who
10 'Beauty Bill of a Lifetime', *Daily Mail*, 21 February 2011.
11 'The Lipstick Effect', *Journal of Personality and Social Psychology*, 28 May 2012.
12 *Open Democracy*, 6 March 2012, http://www.opendemocracy.net/5050/kate-donald/feminisation-of-poverty-and-myth-of-welfare-queen
13 T. A. Judge and D. M. Cable, 'When It Comes to Pay, Do the Thin Win?', http://www.ncbi.nlm.nih.gov/pubmed/20853946
14 http://greatist.com/fitness/15-olympic-inspired-exercises-try-today, 10 August 2012
15 Astounding increase in antidepressant use by Americans, Peter Wehrwein, Contributor, Harvard Health, posted 20 October 2011, 12:46pm,http://www.health.harvard.edu/blog/astounding-increase-in-antidepressant-use-by-americans-201110203624
16 'A Report from Naropa' by Stephen Scobie in *Beats and Rebel Angels: A Tribute to Allen Ginsberg*, Naropa Institute, Boulder, Colorado, 2–9 July 1994, http://www.litkicks.com/Topics/NaropaReport.html
17 http://liesjournal.net/http://libcom.org/library/lies-journal-marxist-feminism

CHAPTER 2: LOST BOYS

1 The obvious answer to which is: yes, of course I'll make you a sandwich. It will be made of the dust of history, and I hope you choke on it.
2 Susan Faludi, *Stiffed: Betrayal of the American Male*, Harper Perennial, New York, 2000.
3 Barbara Ehrenreich, *The Hearts of Men: American Dreams and the Flight from Commitment*, Anchor, New York, 1987.
4 Ibid.
5 Ibid.
6 Simone de Beauvoir, Introduction to *The Second Sex* (1949), translated from the French by H. M. Parshley, Penguin, Harmondsworth, 1953.
7 Emile Durkheim, *Suicide: a Study in Sociology* (1897), The Free Press, New York, 1997.

8 Ibid.

9 Dan Savage, 'It Gets Better', http://www.youtube.com/user/itgetsbetterproject

10 http://www.npr.org/2011/03/23/134628750/dan-savage-for-gay-teens-life-gets-better

11 Tamara A. Lennox, 'Occupy Rape Culture', 5 November 2011, http://thefeministwire.com/2011/11/occupy-rape-culture/

12 NPR.org, 23 March 2011, http://www.theguardian.com/uk/2013/apr/26/anonymous-uk-founder-accused-rape

13 www.bbc.co.uk – 2 May 2013 – Occupy London activist cleared of rape at St Paul's camp.

14 www.zerdredge.com, 27 December 2011.

15 http://www.oneinfourusa.org/statistics.php

16 Jackson Katz, TED Talk, http://www.ted.com/talks/jackson_katz_violence_against_women_it_s_a_men_s_issue.html

CHAPTER 3: ANTICLIMAX

1 See Adam Ant, 'Ligotage' – 'don't say you like it. You're not allowed to like it.'

2 http://www.bbc.co.uk/news/world-us-canada-13320785

3 http://www.apa.org/pi/women/programs/girls/report.aspx

4 Ibid.

5 'legitimate rape' – a phrase made infamous by Congressman Todd Akin, http://www.nytimes.com/2012/08/20/us/politics/todd-akin-provokes-ire-with-legitimate-rape-comment.html?_r=0

6 Shere Hite, *The Hite Report*, Collier Macmillan, New York, 1976.

7 Cuckold's defence removed from statutes, http://news.bbc.co.uk/1/hi/uk/7528652.stm

8 For example, the Irish Republic.

9 Cynthia A. Freeland, *Feminist Interpretations of Aristotle*, Pennsylvania State University Press, 1998.

10 Forced counselling law, http://www.reproductivereview.org/index.php/site/article/184/

11 www.rapecrisis.org.uk/statistics2.php.

12 Rousseau 'the appearance of correct behavior must be among

women's duties, 1762 Jean-Jacques Rousseau, *Emile*, Book V, p. 358.

13 Jean-Jacques Rousseau, *Emile*, Book V, p. 358.

14 Katie Roiphe, *Newsweek*, 16 April 2012, http://www.thedailybeast.com/newsweek/2012/04/15/working-women-s-fantasies.html

15 Valerie Tanico, Alternet, 25 July 2005 – http://www.alternet.org/america-place-where-doctors-need-bullet-proof-vests-protect-themselves-christian-fundamentalists

16 Andrew Goldman, 'Our Lady of Contraception', *New York Times*, 22 June 2012.

17 Dan Almira, *NY* Magazine, 'Rick Santorum Preaches Evils of Contraception' – http://nymag.com/daily/intelligencer/2012/02/rick-santorum-contraception-birth-control-sex.html

18 Jean-Jacques Rousseau, *Emile*, Book V, p. 358.

19 Caitlin Moran, *How to be a Woman*, Ebury Press, 2012.

20 http://www.alternet.org/sex-amp-relationships/adolescents-arent-having-much-sex-despite-all-hype-contrary

21 Of course, a great many women are both of these things.

22 DWP 2011, 'Households below Average Income: an Analysis of the Income Distribution 1994–5/2009–11'.

23 Witness the derision heaped on the family of 'Honey Boo Boo' or 'Octomom' in the United States.

24 Ann Rossiter, *Ireland's Hidden Diaspora: The Abortion Trail and the Making of a London-Irish Underground*, 1980-2000 (New York: IASC Publishing, 2009).

25 According to the UN *World Abortion Policies 2011* publication, abortion in case of rape and incest is accepted in 49% of countries, but only in a third for socio-economic reasons.

26 For example, Spain and Republic of Ireland

27 For example, Pope Francis – http://worldnews.nbcnews.com/_news/2014/01/13/22288490-pope-francis-makes-toughest-remarks-yet-on-horrific-abortion?lite

28 This is called 'post-abortion syndrome' and has no medical basis. See 'The Post Abortion Syndrome Myth'. http://www.prochoice.org/about_abortion/myths/post_abortion_syndrome.html

29 Rape, Abuse and Incest Nation Network statistics, www.rainn.org/statistics

30 Ibid.

31 Jessica Valedi, *The Nation*, on Woody Allen, January 2014, http://www.thenation.com/blog/178203/choosing-comfort-over-truth-what-it-means-defend-woody-allen

CHAPTER 4: CYBERSEXISM

1 Donna Haraway. See Interview with Donna J. Haraway, *Cyborg Manifesto*, 1987.

2 Ibid.

3 Ibid.

4 http://www.newstatesman.com/blogs/helen-lewis-hasteley/*2011/11/* comments-rape-abuse-women.

5 http://madelineashby.com/?p=1198

6 http://www.dissentmagazine.org/article/girl-geeks-and-boy-kings

7 Tanith Carey, *Where Has My Little Girl Gone?*, Lion Books, Oxford, 2011), https://www.getsafeonline.org/safeguarding-children/#.Uw26z_l_tN8

8 http://www.telegraph.co.uk/women/womens-life/10489265/Domestic-violence-death-toll-will-rise-due-to-funding-cuts.html

9 http://www.telegraph.co.uk/culture/tvandradio/9816860/Vile-online-misogyny-is-enough-to-put-women-off-appearing-in-public-says-Mary-Beard.html

10 Helen Lewis, 'What it's like to be a victim of Don't Start Me Off's internet hate mob', *New Statesman*, 27 January 2013.

11 Ben Dowell, 'Mary Beard row: website owner says sorry but accuses friends of "trolling"', *Guardian*, 25 January 2013.

12 Cristina Odone, 'Mary Beard is clever. So how can she be cross that Question Time viewers mocked her looks?', *Daily Telegraph*, 22 January 2013.

13 Germaine Greer, *The Female Eunuch*, Farrar, Straus & Giroux, New York, 1970, p. 263.

14 http://www.feministfrequency.com/2013/11/ms-male-character-tropes-vs-women/

15 http://www.newstatesman.com/internet/2013/08/diary-internet-trolls-twitter-rape-threats-and-putting-jane-austen-our-banknotes

16 http://www.independent.co.uk/voices/commentators/laurie-penny-a-womans-opinion-is-the-miniskirt-of-the-internet-6256946.html
17 http://www.newstatesman.com/blogs/internet/2012/07/what-online-harassment-looks
18 Interview with Maha Rafi Atal.
19 Katherine Losse, *The Boy Kings: A Journey Into the Heart of the Social Network*, Free Press, New York, 2005.
20 Ibid.
21 http://www.wired.com/opinion/2013/05/fa_thompson/
22 Author interview; see also Katherine Losse, *The Boy Kings*.
23 http://www.cracked.com/article_19785_5-ways-modern-men-are-trained-to-hate-women_p2.html
24 Ibid.
25 http://coalescent.dreamwidth.org/431233.html
26 http://www.wired.com/opinion/2013/11/silicon-valley-isnt-a-meritocracy-and-the-cult-of-the-entrepreneur-holds-people-back/
27 Cordelia Fine, *Delusions of Gender: The Real Science Behind Sex Differences*, Icon Books, London, 2009.
28 Simon Baron-Cohen, *The Essential Difference*, Penguin Press, London, 2004; see also http://www.theguardian.com/education/2003/apr/17/research.highereducation
29 http://gawker.com/tag/violentacrez

CHAPTER 5: LOVE AND LIES

1 http://www.dazeddigital.com/artsandculture/article/17926/1/what-doris-taught-us
2 Tiqqun et al., *Introduction to Civil War*, MIT Press (2010).
3 bell hooks, *All About Love*, Harper Perennial, London, 2001.
4 http://www.avclub.com/article/the-bataan-death-march-of-whimsy-case-file-1-emeli-15577
5 Douglas Rushkoff, *Present Shock: When Everything Happens Now*, Current, New York, 2013.
6 Scott Neustadter, *500 Days of Summer* (2009).

7 http://www.huffingtonpost.com/2012/07/18/zoe-kazan-ruby-sparks-manic-pixie-dream-girl_n_1683841.html
8 Kate Zambreno, *Heroines*, Semiotext(e), Los Angeles, 2012.
9 The World's Women 2010 – Trends and Statistics, UN Report.
10 Eli J. Finkel, 'The All or Nothing Marriage', *New York Times*, 14 February 2014.
11 'Beyond Gay Marriage', *Nation*, 29 June 2005.
12 Samhita Mukhopadhyay, *Outdated : Why Dating Is Ruining Your Life*, Seal Press, Berkeley, 2012.
13 Ibid.
14 http://www.telegraph.co.uk/news/politics/10172627/Most-children-will-be-born-out-of-wedlock-by-2016.html
15 Ibid.
16 Alexandra Kollontai, 'The Aims and Worth of My Life', preface to *The Autobiography of a Sexually Emancipated Communist Woman*, translated by Salvator Attansio, Herder and Herder, New York, 1971; http://www.marxists.org/archive/kollonta/1926/autobiography.htm
17 http://www.guernicamag.com/features/john_berger_7_15_11/
18 Emma Goldman, 'Marriage and Love', in *Anarchism and Other Essays*, Mother Earth Publishing Association, New York, 1910.

Bibliography

Anders, Charlie Jane, 'Mama Cash: Buying and Selling Genders', in Joel Schalit, ed., *The Anti-Capitalism Reader: Imagining a Geography of Opposition*, Akashic Books, New York, 2002

Banyard, Kat, *The Equality Illusion: The Truth about Women and Men Today*, Faber & Faber, London, 2010

Barker, Meg, *Rewriting The Rules: An Integrative Guide to Love, Sex and Relationships*, Routledge, New York, 2012

de Beauvoir, Simone, *The Second Sex*, Bantam Books, New York, 1961

Black Girl Dangerous, http://www.blackgirldangerous.org/

Black, Hannah, 'Value, Measure, Love', *New Inquiry*, 30 July 2012

—, 'K in Love', *New Inquiry*, 14 February 2013

Bordo, Susan, *Unbearable Weight: Feminism, Western Culture, and the Body*, University of California Press, Berkeley, 1993

Bornstein, Kate, *My Gender Workbook: How to Become a Real Man, a Real Woman, the Real You, or Something Else Entirely*, Routledge, Oxford, 1997

Bornstein, Kate, *A Queer and Pleasant Danger*, Beacon Press, Boston, 2012

Butler, Judith, *Gender Trouble: Feminism and the Subversion of Identity*, Routledge, Oxford, 1989

Butler, Octavia, *Bloodchild: And Other Stories*, Four Walls Eight Windows, New York, 1995

Chapadjiev, Sabrina, ed., *Live Through This: On Creativity and Self-Destruction*, Seven Stories Press, New York, 2008

Chen, Ching-In, ed., *The Revolution Starts at Home: A Reader on Activism and Intimate Abuse*, South End Press, Cambridge, MA, 2011

Coates, Ta-Nehisi, *The Beautiful Struggle: A Father, Two Sons, and an Unlikely Road to Manhood*, Spiegel & Grau, New York, 2008

Collins, Suzanne, *The Hunger Games*, Scholastic Press, New York, 2008

Cyborgology, http://thesocietypages.org/cyborgology/

Davis, Angela Y., *Women, Race and Class*, Random House, New York, 1981

Deleuze, Gilles and Guattari, Félix, *Anti-Oedipus: Capitalism and Schizophrenia*, Editions de Minuit, Paris, 1972

Despentes, Virginie, *King Kong Theory*, Serpents Tail, London, 2009

Dworkin, Andrea, *Intercourse*, Free Press, New York, 1987

—, *Heartbreak: The Political Memoir of a Feminist Militant*, Basic Books, New York, 2002

Dziuria, Jen, 'Bullish', http://www.getbullish.com/

Easton, Dossie, *The Ethical Slut: A Guide to Infinite Sexual Possibilities*, Greenery Press, Emeryville, CA, 1997

Ehrenreich, Barbara, *The Hearts of Men: American Dreams and the Flight from Commitment*, Anchor Books, New York, 1983

Feministing, http://feministing.com/

Firestone, Shulamith, *The Dialectic of Sex: The Case for the Feminist Revolution*, William Morrow & Co., New York, 1970

Fisher, Mark, *Capitalist Realism: Is There No Alternative?*, Zero Books, Ropley, 2009

Friedan, Betty, *The Feminine Mystique*, W. W. Norton & Co., New York, 1963

Foucault, Michel, *The History of Sexuality 1: An Introduction*, Gallimard, Paris, 1976

—, *The History of Sexuality 2: The Use of Pleasure*, Gallimard, Paris, 1984

Goldman, Emma, *Anarchism and Other Essays*, Mother Earth Publishing Association, New York, 1910

—, *Living My Life*, Knopf, New York, 1931

Gira Grant, Melissa, *Playing The Whore: The Work of Sex Work*, Verso, New York, 2014

—, ed., *Coming and Crying*, Glass Houses, New York, 2010

Graeber, David, *Debt: The First 5,000 Years*, Melville House, New York, 2011

—, *The Democracy Project: A History, a Crisis, a Movement*, Allen Lane, London, 2012

Greer, Germaine, *The Female Eunuch*, Flamingo, London, 1970

Hakim, Katherine, *Honey Money: The Power of Erotic Capital*, Allen Lane, London, 2011

Haraway, Donna, 'A Cyborg Manifesto: Science, Technology, and Socialist-Feminism in the Late Twentieth Century', *Socialist Review*, San Francisco, 1985

Hite, Shere, *The Hite Report*, Collier Macmillan, New York, 1976

Holloway, John, *Change the World Without Taking Power: The Meaning of Revolution Today*, Pluto Press, London, 2002

hooks, bell, *Wounds of Passion: A Writing Life*, Henry Holt & Co., New York, 1997

—, *Feminism Is for Everybody: Passionate Politics*, South End Press, Cambridge, MA, 2000

—, *All About Love*, Harper Perennial, New York, 2001

—, *We Real Cool: Black Men and Masculinity*, Routledge, Oxford, 2003

Hornbacher, Marya, *Wasted: A Memoir of Anorexia and Bulimia*, HarperCollins, New York, 1997

The Invisible Committee, *The Coming Insurrection*, La Fabrique, Paris, 2007

James, Selma, *Sex, Race and Class: The Perspective of Winning: A Selection of Writings 1952–2011*, PM Press, Oakland, CA, 2012

Jones, Rhian E., *Clampdown: Pop-Cultural Wars on Class and Gender*, Zero Books, Ropley, 2013

Kipnis, Laura, *Against Love: A Polemic*, Pantheon, New York, 2003

Kollontai, Alexandra, *Red Love*, Seven Arts, New York, 1927

—, *The Autobiography of a Sexually Emancipated Communist Woman*, Herder and Herder, New York, 1971

Le Guin, Ursula K., *The Left Hand Of Darkness*, Walker & Company, New York, 1969

Lenin's Tomb, http://www.leninology.com/

Lessing, Doris, *The Golden Notebook*, Harper Perennial, New York, 1962

Lies Journal – A Journal of Materialist Feminism, http://liesjournal.net/

Losse, Kate, *The Boy Kings: A Journey into the Heart of the Social Network*, Free Press, New York, 2012

Lunch, Lydia, *Lydia Lunch*, Re/Search Publications, San Francisco, 2013

Martin, Courtney E., *Perfect Girls, Starving Daughters: The Frightening New Normality of Hating Your Body*, Free Press, New York, 2007

Mason, Paul, *Why It's Still Kicking Off Everywhere*, Verso, London, 2012

Meinhof, Ulrike, *Everybody Talks about the Weather . . . We Don't: The Writings of Ulrike Meinhof*, Seven Stories Press, New York, 2008

Metcalfe, Andy, ed., *Sexuality of Men*, Pluto Press, London, 1985

Moran, Caitlin, *How to Be a Woman*, Ebury Press, London, 2011

Quinn Norton's Feminist Series at 'Medium', https://medium.com/@quinnnorton

Orbach, Susie, *Fat Is A Feminist Issue*, Paddington Press, New York, 1978

—, *Bodies*, Picador, London, 2009

Pateman, Carole, *The Sexual Contract*, Stanford University Press, Stanford, 1988

Power, Nina, *One Dimensional Woman*, Zero Books, Ropley, 2009

Prickett, Sarah Nicole, 'Where Are All the Women?', *Vice*, 9 February 2013

Riding Jackson, Laura, *The Word Woman and Other Related Writings*, Persea Books, New York, 1993

Rose, Gillian, *Love's Work: A Reckoning with Life*, Random House, New York, 1995

Rosin, Hanna, *The End Of Men: And the Rise of Women*, Riverhead, New York, 2012

Rossiter, Ann, *Ireland's Hidden Diaspora: The 'Abortion Trail' and the Making of a London–Irish Underground, 1980–2000*, Inter-Agency Standing Committee Publishing, IASC, 2009

Sandberg, Sheryl, *Lean In*, Knopf, New York, 2013

Scott, James C., *Seeing Like a State: How Certain Schemes to Improve the Human Condition Have Failed*, Yale University Press, New Haven, 1998

Serano, Julia, *Whipping Girl: A Transsexual Woman on Sexism and the Scapegoating of Femininity*, Seal Press, Berkeley, 2007

Shirky, Clay, *Here Comes Everyone: The Power of Organizing Without Organizations*, Penguin Press, London, 2008

Slaughter, Anne-Marie, 'Why Women Still Can't Have It All', *Atlantic*, 13 July 2012

Sontag, Susan, *On Photography*, Farrar, Strauss & Giroux, New York, 1977

Stross, Charles, *Glasshouse*, Ace Books, New York, 2006

Susann, Jacqueline, *Valley of The Dolls*, Random House, New York, 1961

Tea, Michelle, ed., *Without A Net: The Female Experience of Growing Up Working Class*, Seal Press, Berkeley, 2004

The F Word, http://www.thefword.org.uk/

Tiger Beatdown, http://tigerbeatdown.com/

Turner, Jenny, 'As Many Pairs of Shoes as She Wants', *London Review of Books*, Vol. 33 No. 24, 2011

Valenti, Jessica, *The Purity Myth: How America's Obsession with Virginity is Hurting Young Women*, Seal Press, Berkeley, 2009

Weeks, Kathi, *The Problem with Work: Feminism, Marxism, Antiwork Politics, and Postwork Imaginaries*, Duke University Press Books, Durham, 2011

Weigel, Moira and Ahern, Mal, 'Further Materials Toward a Theory of the Man-Child', *New Inquiry*, 9 July 2013

Willis, Ellen, *No More Nice Girls: Countercultural Essays*, Wesleyan University Press, Middletown, 1992

Winterson, Jeanette, *Written on the Body*, Jonathan Cape, New York, 1992

Wolf, Naomi, *The Beauty Myth: How Images of Beauty Are Used Against Women*, Random House, Toronto, 1990

Zambreno, Kate, *Heroines*, Semiotext(e), Los Angeles, 2012

Index

NOTE ON THE TYPE

The text of this book is set in Bembo. This type was first used in 1495 by the Venetian printer Aldus Manutius for Cardinal Bembo's *De Aetna*, and was cut for Manutius by Francesco Griffo. It was one of the types used by Claude Garamond (1480–1561) as a model for his Romain de l'Université, and so it was the forerunner of what became standard European type for the following two centuries. Its modern form follows the original types and was designed for Monotype in 1929.